DATE DUE

			PRINTED IN U.S.A.

picasso

picasso

Text by
FRANCK ELGAR

LEON AMIEL PUBLISHER
NEW YORK

Published by
LEON AMIEL PUBLISHER
NEW YORK, 1974
ISBN Number 8148-0592-2
© 1974 SPADEM
Printed in Italy

Pablo (1881-1973), Spanish painter, born in Malaga. Although he participated in all the adventures of French painting for half a century, Picasso remained inalienably Spanish. The sumptuous, tragic and ponderous Spanish legacy he carried within himself, in his thought and his mood, and he squandered it without ever exhausting it. However, to find in his work, his vocabulary, his syntax and his themes solely this composite and sumptuous Spain, nourished on the myths and forms of Oriental civilizations, barbarian contributions, Greek and Gothic reminiscences, would be a vast oversimplification. In the formation of his genius it was the Spain of Góngora and Goya, of the baroque architect Gaudi, of catalan anarchism and insurrectionism, a very special Spain, ardent, subversive, violent, passionate, that played the most important part. Be this as it may, no foreign artist working in France allowed himself to be less absorbed by the customs and spirit of France; no one more asserted his loyalty to his origin. For everything was contradiction in Picasso, his life, his character, his work.

The Blue and Rose Periods

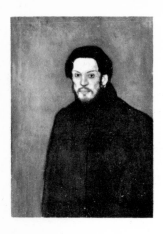

Self-Portrait
Paris 1901

He was born of a Castilian father, José Ruiz Blasco, who was a teacher of drawing, and an Andalusian mother of Majorcan origin, Maria Picasso. At an age when most children are still playing with marbles, he had already painted pictures worthy of figuring in a museum. In 1900 he came to Paris. He admired the pictures of Van Gogh and the Montmartre scenes of Toulouse-Lautrec. The latter's influence is noticeable in the paintings he executed at the time, and also in those of the "Blue Period" (1901-1904). Poor and sick people, outcasts of life, were the objects of his attention. These themes, dear to Spain-poverty, solitude, sadness-he took up, but in a spirit influenced by French art and with means refined by contact with Montmartre draughtsmen. He drew single or grouped figures with increasing precision, but he elongated or narrowed them to stress their tragic expression; he painted them almost in monochrome, in a blue tonality, the blue of mystery and night. Picasso was then twenty-three, but already his name was known far beyond the narrow circle of friends who surrounded him. His output was as exceptional in quality as it was prolific and included these well known works: *La Vie* (1903,

Museum of Art, Cleveland), *Poor People on the Seashore* (1903, Chester Dale Collection, National Gallery, Washington), *Celestine* (1903), *Woman with a Crow* (1904, Museum of Art, Toledo). He established himself in the Bateau-Lavoir, 13 rue Ravignan, in Montmartre, as early as April, 1904, and his studio became a meeting-place where artists and writers worked out the principles of a new aesthetic doctrine. The poets Apollinaire, Max Jacob, André Salmon, Pierre Reverdy, the painters André Derain, Van Dongen and Juan Gris frequented this place or even lived there. After 1907 Georges Braque, introduced to Picasso by Apollinaire, could also be met there. Fernande Olivier has left the following striking portrait of Picasso at this time: "Short, dark, stocky, disturbed, disturbing, with dark, deep, piercing, strange, almost immobile eyes. Awkward movements, a woman's hands, badly dressed, unkempt. A thick lock of hair, black and shiny, gashed the intelligent forehead. Half Bohemian, half workman in dress, he had long hair that swept the collar of his worn coat."

With his "Rose Period" (1905-1906) Picasso seemed to soften, even to mellow. Nudes, itinerant players, harlequins, circus scenes offered him the opportunity of lightening his technique, making his line more supple, accentuating distortions. His works recalled those of the Japanese painters of phantoms. They are char-

Girl on a Ball
Paris 1904

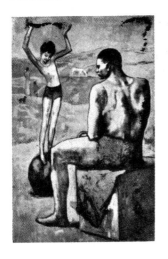

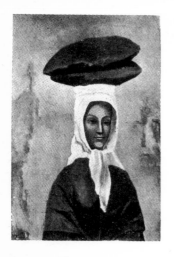

Woman with Loaves
Gosol 1906

acterized by a morbid feeling, something elusive and floating, a rather troubled charm, finally by almost flat forms, sparingly coloured: *The Family of Harlequin* (1905, Lewisohn Collection, New York), *Acrobat Seated with a Child* (1906, Kunsthaus, Zurich), *The Jugglers* (1906, Art Institute, Chicago), *La Toilette* (1906, Albright Art Gallery, Buffalo). But he was not long in reacting. Probably under the influence of Negro and Iberian sculpture, he executed statues, drawings, pictures in which his plastic preoccupations stand out. How could he not be won over by the monstrous distortions of the African fetishes that were then being revealed to Europe? Distortions? Were they not rather invented forms, volumes charged with emotional power?

Be this as it may, Picasso fell under the spell of these primitive works; he certainly admired their sensitivity, rawness, luxuriant vocabulary, and bold abstraction. And when, in 1907, in his dilapidated studio in the Bateau-Lavoir, he showed his disconcerted friends the *Demoiselles d'Avignon* (Museum of Modern Art, New York), a page of history had been turned. The composition of this famous canvas lacks unity, the colour is hard and dry, the figures gesticulate, have no relief. But the lines, the angles, the slope of the planes, announced a new direction in modern painting. The Cubist revolution was

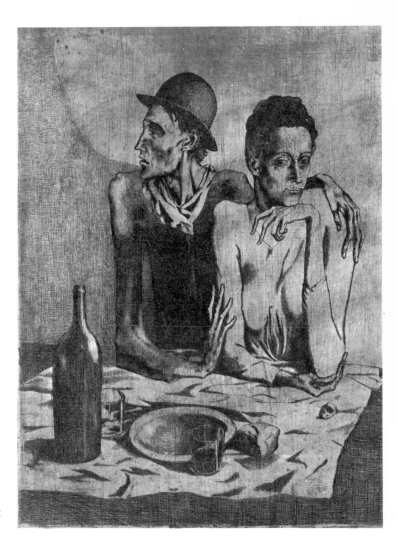

The Frugal Repast
Paris 1904

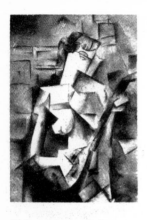

Girl with a Mandoline
Paris 1910

not far off. The *Demoiselles d'Avignon* is not only a picture, it is also an event, a date, a starting-point, as much as were in other times the *Mystic Lamb* of the Van Eycks, the *Battles* of Uccello, *Dante's Barque* of Delacroix.

The Cubist Revolution

Fauvism was already drawing its last breath. In it the century had sown its wild oats, but had pulled itself together rather quickly, and the artist, sobered, had begun thinking. Confined in his studio, he attentively observed the objects that surrounded him, the table, the decanter, the glass, the package of tobacco, the newspaper. He observed them with so penetrating an eye that they appeared unknown to him. He entered into them as the novelist enters into his characters. He settled into them with the aid of a sympathy that was neither love nor passion but total consent and total respect. Thereupon things revealed to him their form, their structure, their top, their inside, their underside. When he represented them with his new vision, Cubism was born. Gauguin was deserted for Cézanne. The real was rediscovered and essentially, in the real, volume and space. A prey to his contradictions, Picasso saw in this transcendence of realism a means of resolving them. He countered the sensualism of the Fauves by an intellectualism that writers were undertaking to explain and encourage at the same moment. As early as 1908 he assumed leadership of the movement with Braque. The question for them was to introduce the illusion of volume on a plane surface without resorting to modelling, chiaroscuro, linear perspective and other outmoded conventions. They succeeded in doing so through the breakdown of planes and representation of the object under several angles simultaneously. From then on they painted not what they saw but what they represented to themselves through analysis. In 1911 Cubism ceased to be analytic; it renounced contemplation of Nature and drifted toward an authoritarian conceptualism. At last tamed and dismantled, the object was subordinated to forms imagined *a priori*.

While their companions went off in other directions, Picasso and Braque exploited their discoveries. The Cubist adventure was like a dazzling conquest of unknown lands, each painting was a step forward from the last and anticipated the next. His new manner enabled Picasso between 1908 and 1915 to produce works with a hitherto unsuspected logic of composition. The portraits of *Ambroise Vollard* (1910, Pushkin Museum, Moscow), and *D.H. Kahnweiler*

Violin and Glass
Paris 1913

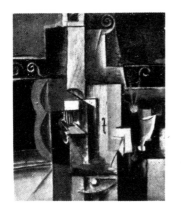

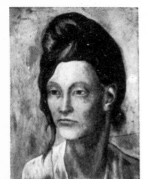

Head of the Acrobat's Wife
Paris 1904

Seated Woman 1948

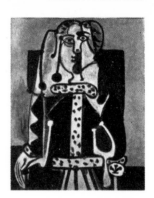

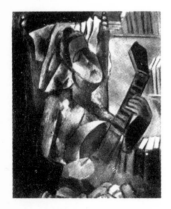

Woman with a Mandoline
Paris 1909

Jacqueline Roque
Vallauris 1954

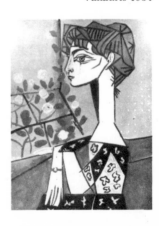

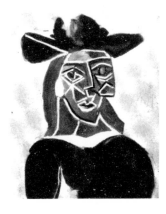

Woman with a Hat 1939

(1910, Art Institute, Chicago), the *Aficionado* (1912, Kunstmuseum, Basel), the *Card Players* (1914, Museum of Modern Art, New York), and the *Harlequin* of 1915 (ibid.), illustrate well the distance he had travelled. The same audacity in the process of abstraction and possibly even greater freedom are noticeable in the still-lifes in which the motif of the guitar and violin constantly reappeared. From that point, he created objects and created them freely. He accounted for reality, but by destroying it and substituting for it a subjective reality, autonomous, absolute. The picture became for him an object in itself. Indifferent to light, he concentrated all his faculties upon the transposed expression of forms, in order that the forms might suggest to the spectator images different from their counterparts in the world of appearances. But there came a moment when Cubism lost through its own excesses the strength it had drawn from the excesses of Fauvism. It was a prisoner of still life, of a closed room. It had not opened the door upon life. Impersonality of handling, poverty of colour, bleak and dreary materials. On the other hand, it had restored to drawing and form a necessary and sometimes tyrannical predominance. As a result, painting had returned to linear purity, geometry, exactness of proportions, rigour of composition.

The Charms of Classicism

However, Picasso soon saw the limitations of the doctrine he had been the first to set forth and illustrate. And he who had been its most ardent instigator became its least faithful practitioner. No sooner did he see that he was followed than he took another path. The painter of angles, cubes, geometrical architectures, applied himself to the study of the old masters. This was the period when he worked for the Ballets Russes and executed settings and costumes for *Parade* (1917) and *The Three-Cornered Hat* (1919). He resumed his old themes, acrobats, harlequins, dancers. Then, influenced by Greco-Roman art, he begot a race of giants, of heavy women, drawn and modelled in an entirely classical way (*Three Women at the Fountain*, 1921, Museum of Modern Art, New York). Until 1925 his production was characterized by calm, balance and an exceptional health. One would not believe the same Picasso had practised the technique of the *papier collé* a few years before, nor that in 1921 he had painted *The Three Musicians* (Museum of Modern Art, New York) in the purest tradition of a liberated Cubism. Nevertheless, he who had gathered together on his canvases pieces of newspaper and boxes of

Olga Picasso 1918

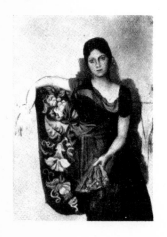

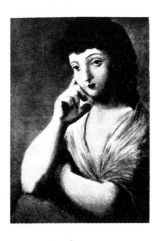

Woman in Blue 1921

matches and indulged in *trompe-l'œil* for love of realism, could not fail to be led to paint like Ingres in moments of relaxation.

On the other hand, a man so torn by different, if not opposing, needs, so sensitive to the currents of his time, so given to every kind of daring, could not remain indifferent to the explorations of Surrealism. Besides, in this insurrectional movement there was a taste for challenge and a will for destruction that could not fail to stimulate his fundamental nihilism. But Surrealist art resorted to means so poor, so worn, so unplastic that Picasso neglected them deliberately. He retained from the experience only the ferment capable of renewing his inspiration. While his countrymen Dali and Miró were obeying the metaphysical-literary directives of the Surrealist poet André Breton, Picasso let crop up in his pictures the madrepores and larvae that stir in the depths of the unconscious (1927-1930). Fantastic forms, without significance, swarmed under his brush. These forms are strongly schematized, feebly coloured, with very dense volumes, that stand out, absurd and comic, in a space without depth (*Standing Swimmer*, 1929; *Seated Swimmer*, 1929). Towards 1932 the straight lines disappeared in favour of long, flexible curves, the summary structures gave way to exuberant arabesque, colour took on a heavy and sensual brilliance. A radiant personality had suddenly irrupted into his life and no form was too audacious or too fantastic to express his passion: *The Dream* (1932, Victor Ganz Collection, New York), *Young Woman with a Mirror* (1932, Museum of Modern Art, New York).

Guernica

Mother and Child 1921

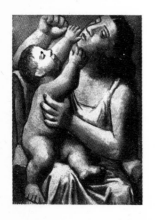

In 1935 the latent expressionism of Picasso reappeared, exasperated by the tragedy that was drenching his motherland with blood. The line twisted or swelled, the colour heightened, the emotion burst out and, at the climax of a pathetic crescendo, reached its paroxysm in *Guernica* (1937, on loan to the Museum of Modern Art, New York). This large composition in black and white is certainly one of his masterpieces, if not his masterpiece. For while he expressed in it the horrors of war in apocalyptic images, for his purpose he called only upon form and contrasts of shadow and light. Instead of describing, as did Goya or Delacroix, for example, a certain military episode or scene of slaughter, Picasso succeeded, for the first

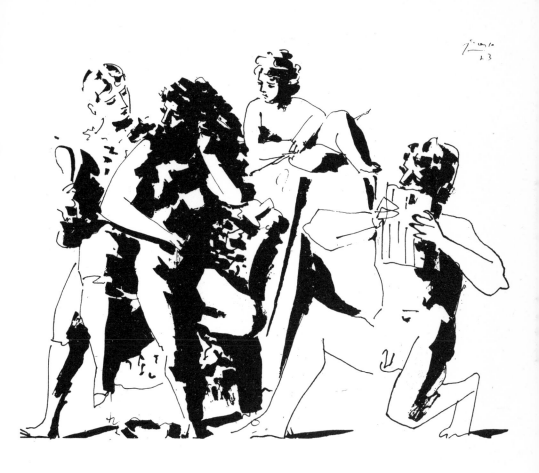

Young Man with Mirror
and Pipes of Pan 1923

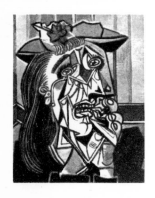

Weeping Woman
Paris 1937

time in the history of Western painting, in terrifying the spectator merely by a plastic transcription of an actual event and convicting him of guilt by combining, with shrewdness and passion, specifically pictorial values. The tragic and the burlesque, sarcasm and pity, imprecation and irony, the palpitation of life and the immobility of death, a tumult of thoughts and emotions spring from this agonizing picture with an intensity that is at the limit of human endurance. After this, Picasso explored courses he had already followed, carrying his investigations ever farther, now casting anchor in the peaceful river of Humanism, now venturing in full sail among Romantic storms. The same year in which he finished *Guernica*, he also painted the extraordinary, overwhelming *Weeping Woman* (Roland Penrose Collection, London) and began the *Seated Women* (1937-1944) series. Sometimes pleasing, more often hideous, with dislocated limbs and atrociously tortured anatomies, they were aggressions against the human figure and, in their own way, were a witness to the dark tragedy that humanity was suffering at the time. The war did not interrupt the frenzied tempo of his work, in fact, he painted some of his least questionable successes: *L'Aubade* (1942, Musée National d'Art Moderne, Paris), *Still-life with a Bull's Skull* (1942, Kunstsammlung Nordrhein-Westfalen, Düsseldorf),

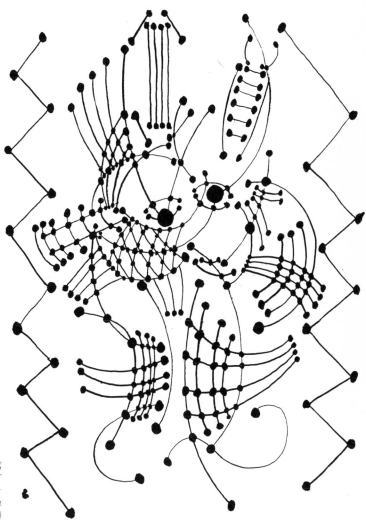

Ink drawing
Illustration for
Balzac's *Le Chef-
d'œuvre inconnu*
(Vollard 1931)

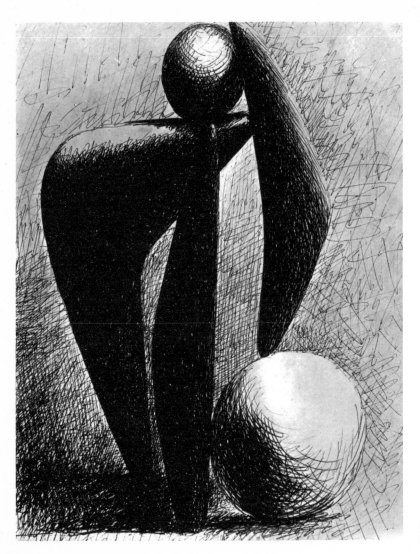

Indian Ink
drawing
Dinard 1928

The Tomato Plant (1944), which was a triumph of equilibrium and contained energy. The *Charnel House* (1945, Walter P. Chrysler Jr. Collection, New York) in contrast is a dramatic composition. He produced numerous lithographs during the same period and worked nearly every day at the Mourlot workshops.

On Mediterranean Shores

In July 1946, he left Paris and divided his time between Golfe-Juan and the Musée d'Antibes, where he was provided with a studio. He painted an impressive number of works there in four months, which he donated to the museum. They are based on the ancient myths and magic beliefs brought in former times to the western shores of the Mediterranean by Greek sailors. In the autumn of 1948, he went to live in Vallauris, where he devoted himself to ceramics with such enthusiasm that he brought new life to a declining art. The birth of his son, Claude, in 1947, and his daughter, Paloma, in 1949, inspired the paintings of motherhood and portraits of his children that are full of tenderness. He painted, engraved, sculptured and made pottery, all at the same time. Decorative painting attracted him and in 1952 he began and completed the two large panels of *War and Peace* for a disused chapel in Vallauris. Six years later, he painted a mural for the UNESCO building in Paris (*The Fall of Icarus*). While continuing his sculpture and lithography, from time to time he painted landscapes, still-lifes and portraits (*Portrait of Hélène Parmelin*, 1952; *Portraits of Sylvette*, 1954; *Portrait of Jacqueline*, 1954) and all this with his usual impetuosity and an unusual love of life. And whatever his subjects, his motifs, he always metamorphosed them, gave them a life similar to his own, an ill-restrained violence, a desperate note, something wild, troubled, disquieting. He was curious and unsatisfied, irritating and fascinating, generous and avaricious with his feelings, laden with fame and wealth, continuing nevertheless to work like a slave, the slave of his impatient genius, but also the master of his forces, of his faculties, prodigiously active, never at rest, knowing no weariness, always seeking in the world an ever-elusive joy and meeting only with anguish, doubt, fury. The age he seemed to be was not his real age. He worked, conceived, felt, hated and loved as at twenty. It is therefore difficult to study his production without studying his life, so inex-

Woman in an Armchair the Dream Paris 1932

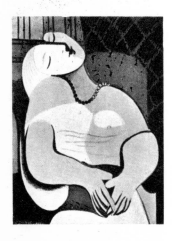

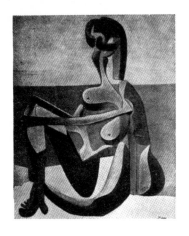

Seated Bather 1930

tricably are the two mixed. All the facts, all the events in which he had been an actor or a witness are registered in his various works. He nourished his art with his loves, his contempts, his torments, his whims, revolts, his presumptions, not without complacency, not without trickery, with a sometimes embarrassing insistence. An heir of the Humanist tradition, an individualist by temperament, an anarchist by race, his actions and reactions were always unpredictable, sudden and brutal. An unbeliever, he believed only in himself. A revolutionary, he baffled his followers. Always the contradiction.

The Genius of Contradictions

There is neither unity nor continuity nor stability in his work, as there was none in his life. Inconstant, multiple, fiery and irascible, amiable or insolent, sincere or affected, charming or uncivil, he could be one or another according to his mood or the moment, and yet remain unfailingly true to a single passion: freedom. He wanted to be entirely free, free to remake

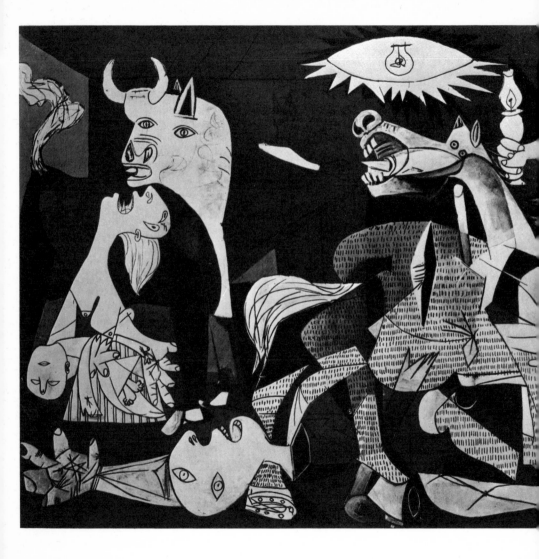

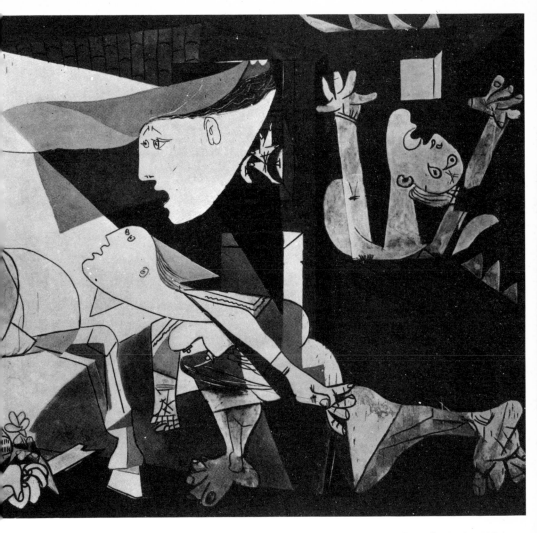

Guernica Paris 1937
The Museum of Modern Art, New York

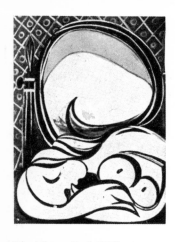

The Mirror Paris 1932

the world to his liking, free to exercise his omnipotence-no rules, no conventions, no prejudice. From Naturalism to Expressionism, from Expressionism to Classicism, from Classicism to Romanticism, then to Realism and to Abstraction, to revert to Naturalism and resume his indefatigable quest, grace alternating with horror, elegance with the monstrous, he went to and fro, he began again, remaining an inveterate baroque in spite of his incarnations. When he wanted to be classical, he startled less and did not move. He was too individualistic, too anxious to surprise and hurt, too hostile to all restraint and to any serene vision of the universe, to put up with limitations, discipline, humilities. Freedom alone suited him, absolute freedom, even if it had to take on the forms of the bizarre, of chaos, of the hideous. Picasso was a baroque by atavism, by principle, by inclination. And as one gets used to everything, to the exceptional, to extravagance, to strangeness, even to horror, he was naturally led to outdo his previous violence; hence his immoderateness and his recklessness, but hence also the percussive force of each of his creations, his violent drawing, aggressive forms, hurried and tense composition. It is by virtue of this that he dazzles, upsets, intoxicates and convinces. Electricity runs along his line; there is dynamite in the hollow of his objects.

Prodigious as his vitality was, Picasso does not express happiness, hope, or joy of living, but mostly an incurable disquiet, the drama of man at grips with Nature, of man in revolt against his destiny—his own drama. When he is playful or facetious, when he wants to please or to charm, it is rare that the mask succeeds in concealing entirely the wan face of Death. His laugh is more like a sneer, his exultations sound like blasphemies, his banter like sarcasm. Widsom, renunciation, serenity, naturalness, he had none of these in him. It was with his resources alone that he wanted to substitute for the world of permanence his personal and therefore fragile, everthreatened world. Picasso was an individual who strives to extend the borders of his empire in order to go farther, ever farther; who tends to absorb everything, no doubt because he needs to be absorbed himself. Is there today an artist more profoundly an innovator, more determined to reject the fictions and forms of the past? Picasso was, in fact, the last representative, the most passionate, the most terrible, of the Greco-Latin tradition. He was the prodigal descendant of Goya, Velasquez, Michelangelo, Uccello. One will, then, perhaps understand why this paradox should have resounded with such painful echoes in a body of work with which no other can be compared.

Persistent Youthfulness

As Picasso grew older, his painterly activity, his enormous vitality, showed no signs of weakening. He was fond of borrowing themes from famous pictures which, with a remarkable creative unselfconsciousness, he interpreted in his own way. After drawing his inspiration from Greco and Courbet in 1950, he turned to Delacroix in 1955 (*Women of Algiers*) and Velasquez in 1957 (a series of fifty-eight variations on *Las Meninas*, which the artist donated to the Picasso Museum in Barcelona). At the same time, he executed the series of *Ateliers* (1955-1956), thirty-five pictures that freely interpret the setting of "La Californie."

In 1958, seeking solitude and isolation, Picasso bought the chateau of Vauvenargues, an austere building that stands at the foot of the Montagne Sainte-Victoire. No sooner had he settled there the following year than he began a dazzling series of lino-cuts while continuing his usual output of drawings, paintings and sculptures. The painting then consisted of canvases that were cut out and polychromed with an unbridled fantasy. During the same period he painted about a hundred watercolours, which can be grouped under the title of *Romancero du Picador*. They vividly bring

Boats on the Beach
Juan-les-Pins 1937

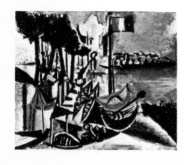

to life the Spain of corridas, aficionados and senoritas wearing mantillas. Between February, 1960 and 1961, it was Manet's *le Déjeuner sur l'Herbe* that provided his inexhaustible imagination with a theme.

In April, 1961, he left the chateau of Vauvenargues, which twelve years later became his final resting place, and settled at Mougins in the small farmhouse Notre-Dame-de-Vie that he had just bought. It was there that he spent the remaining years of his life, years in which he continued to give proof of his persistent youthfulness and of his ability to renew himself. Even at the age of ninety, or almost, he would sometimes produce three or four pictures in the same day and a dozen drawings. For instance, the 23 pictures and 138 drawings of the *Déjeuner sur l'Herbe* were all executed in eighteen months, and 347 engravings that express a ferocious eroticism and an infallible mastery were completed in less than seven months, from May 13 to October 5, 1968—when he was eighty-seven.

In 1962 he devoted himself again to ceramics, although he had never really stopped working on ceramics since his first work in that medium at Vallauris. Now he created many series of hollow bricks and of tiles decorated with human faces (especially Jacqueline's). He also did many tiles depicting scenes inspired by the

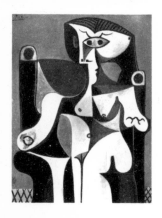

Seated Woman
(Black and White)
Moungins 1962

licentious decorations on Greek vases. That same year Picasso interpreted *The Rape of the Sabines* by David; his interpretation is marked by a violence so intense it is almost unbearable. This was followed by new pictorial and graphic variations on the same theme done in a very short span of time. What Picasso wanted was to make visible, both for himself and for others, the supreme proof of his spiritual and gestural agility. Undoubtedly, too, he wanted to enjoy —with that forever poignant complacency of old men who refuse to accept their decline—the flattering illusion of being able to compete with the youngest of his contemporaries.

The fact remains, however, that everything he did from then on strikes us as being an arrogant challenge to death. Remembrances of the Spanish tragedy, the monstrous anatomies of *Seated Women*, alternate in his work with images that are now attractive, now moving, such as the variations on the *Painter and His Model*, the ironic "espagnolades" on the theme of *Susanna and the Old Men*, the bucolic celebrations, the poetic pastoral scenes, the themes devoted to motherhood, the touching figures of children, and the familiar characters of the matador, the hidalgo and the pipe-smoker, painted in a slightly mocking way.

One thing is clear: there are no more ambitious drawings or truly decisive initiatives, such as the *Demoiselles d'Avignon*, *Guernica* or *War and Peace*. It is as if, before departing, the Master of Mougins had wished to hastily recapitulate and bring together all the themes and methods by means of which he expressed his genius for more than sixty years. The two hundred paintings, dated from September, 1970 to June, 1972, which were exhibited with his approval at the Palais des Papes in Avignon during the summer of 1973, confirm this. But Picasso died only a few weeks before the opening of the exhibit. For the countless admirers who came from all over to visit it, it represented the final farewell to the world of this powerful creator who, until the end, was able to escape from the maledictions of age and seize life with the same passion that inspired him when he was twenty years old.

A Master Without Heirs

His output was huge. It has to be accepted as it is, with its failings, its lightning-flashes, its imperfections, its grandeurs. In it one can count many sketches, experiments without

Still-Life with Guitar
Paris 1942

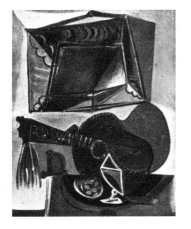

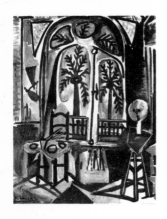

The Studio of
« La Californie »
Cannes 1955

conclusion, but also ardent confessions, incontestable successes. It is not a question of masterpieces; Picasso was never concerned with producing eternal masterpieces. As a result, he always appeared indifferent to the materials he employed. He drew and painted on anything: a paper tablecloth, cardboard, wood or plywood, fibrocement. He did not concern himself with the preparation of his canvases, the quality of his colours, the improvement of his tools. As a sculptor he used earth, wood, cloth, broken pieces of hardware, which he often covered with wide strokes of the brush. But the waste of his abundant production can be forgotten for his having been capable of creating works like *Woman in Green* (1909, Stedelijk Van Abbemuseum, Eindhoven), *The Accordeon Player* (1911, Solomon R. Guggenheim Museum, New York), *Ma Jolie* (1914, Private Collection, Paris), *The Three Musicians* (1921), those fine examples of Cubism; *Guernica* (1937), *War and Peace* (1952), fine flowers of Expressionism; *Mandoline and Guitar, or the Open Window* (1924, Solomon R. Guggenheim Museum, New York), *Still-life with Antique Head* (1925, Musée National d'Art Moderne, Paris), *Still-life with an Enamel Saucepan* (1945, ibid.), and the great paintings of the Musée d'Antibes. Never was technique for him an end in itself, despite his fabulous dexterity. But never did such dexterity stop him from exploring new paths, nor did his boldness ever give way to virtuosity. He did not scorn effect, but to obtain it he committed himself entirely, with his sincerity and his guile, his resolution and his uncertainty, his confessions and his malice, his discoveries and his artifices.

His finds have often been taken up by the new generation. It is certainly easy to discern here and there in contemporary painting a sign, a form, a technique that bears his stamp. But these are superficial borrowings, fragmented and unassimilated imitations. For art, like Picasso's individuality, is autonomous, incommunicable, intransmissible, a closed world. "I do not search, I find," he once announced. His person cannot serve as a model, his life as an example, or his work as a lesson. Picassos are not born in every century. And who does not feel that without him our century would have been flatter, duller, less worth living in?

We must be grateful for his boldness and inventiveness, and the shocks he administers to sluggish ways of thinking and seeing. He was the most original creative genius of our time.

FRANK ELGAR.

Translated by
Wade Stevenson

BIOGRAPHY

1881
Birth at Malaga. His father José Ruiz Blasco, a Basque, taught drawing at the School of Art and Technology. His mother, Maria Picasso, whose name he adopted in 1901, was Andalusian.

1891
The family moved to Barcelona, where Picasso's father who showed no interest in his academic subjects, helped his father to paint. His father solemnly presented his palette, brushes and colors to his son and gave up painting.

1895-1896
The family moved Barcelona, where Picass's father taught at the School of Fine Art. Pablo passed brilliantly the entrance examination to the advanced class at the school.

1897
Picasso painted *Visiting the Sick* (better known as *Knowledge and Charity*), which received an honorable mention at the arts exhibition at Madrid. In October, he was admitted to the Royal Academy at San Fernando, which, in fact, he did not attend.

1898-1899
After this stay in Madrid, Picasso returned to Barce-

lona. There he was a frequent visitor to the cabaret of "El Quatre Gats", the meeting place of a turbulent crowd of young intellectuals and artists.

1900
First visit to Paris with Casagemas. Picasso met Berthe Weill and Manach, a Catalan industrialist, who was interested in his painting.

1901
On his return to Spain, Picasso founded the review *Arte Joven* at Madrid. It only ran to a few numbers, illustrated by the young artist in a style reminiscent of Steinlen and Toulouse-Lautrec. He held two exhibitions during the year: one at Barcelona at the Sala Parès, the other at Paris at Ambroise Vollard's, rue Laffite.

1902-1903
He traveled several times between Barcelona and Paris, where his new friends included Max Jacob. His paintings at the time were profoundly melancholy and suffused by a blue tone (the Blue Period).

1904
Left Barcelona finally and settled at Paris in Paco Durion's studio, 13 rue Ravignan, in the famous Bateau-Lavoir, that "rendez-vous of poets", where André Salmon and Van Dongen were also living.

1905
Picasso met Guillaume Apollinaire and Fernande Olivier. Her youth and beauty brought new hope into his life and they lived together. A few collectors began coming to his studio and bought some of his first paintings. Gertrude Stein and her brother Leo were among them.

1907
After working for several months on the preliminary drawings and studies, Picasso painted the *Demoiselles d'Avignon*.

1908
The experimental approach of the *Demoiselles d'Avignon* was continued with the same desire to eliminate all detail in a series of landscapes and still lifes. In the same year, he held the famous banquet given in his studio in honor of the Douanier Rousseau.

1909
Summer at Horta de Ebro. As he painted this ideal landscape, shot with light, Picasso recorded the subject from several angles in the same painting and broke the surface into innumerable planes that caught and reflected the light. This was Analytical Cubism. Moved into a new studio, boulevard de Clichy. Braque was his neighbor. The great Russian dealers, Shchukin and Morozov, bought his works, easing his financial difficulties.

1912
A new companion entered Picasso's life, Eva. He introduced letters of the alphabet and papiers collés into his paintings, which marked the beginning of Synthetic Cubism. Left the boulevard de Clichy and moved into an apartment in the boulevard Raspail.

1913-1914
Stayed at Céret with Braque and Juan Gris. War declared when he was at Avignon and he returned to Paris.

1916-1917
Death of Eva. Went to Rome with Jean Cocteau to meet Serge de Diaghilev and prepare the settings and costumes for "Parade", which was performed in Paris in May. He was attracted to a dancer of the company, Olga Koklova, whom he married the following year.

1918

Exhibition at Paul Guillaume's gallery with Henri Matisse. Met Paul Rosenberg at Biarritz.

1919-1920

Sets and costumes for "Tricorne" and "Pulcinella", performed by the Ballets Russes.

1921

Sets and costumes for "Cuadro Flamenco" also performed by Diaghilev's Ballets Russes. Birth of his son Paulo. During a visit to Fontainebleau, he painted the two versions of *Three Musicians*. Exhibition at the Leicester Galleries, London, of about sixty works produced between 1902 and 1919.

1922-1924

Designed two theater sets: Jean Cocteau's "Antigone", performed at the Théâtre de l'Atelier, and "Mercure", performed by the Soirées de Paris directed by the Comte E. de Beaumont.

1925

Révolution Surréaliste No. 4 reproduced the *Demoiselles d'Avignon* and published a long article by André Breton on Picasso, who exhibited with the group at the Galerie Pierre. Painted the *Danse* in the spring during a visit to Monte Carlo with Diaghilev.

1926-1929

Took up sculpture again. Bought the Château de Boisgeloup, near Gisors, which offered him huge areas of studio space. In 1930, was awarded the Carnegie Prize.

1932

Met Marie-Thérèse Walter, who became his companion. Painted a series of *Sleeping Women*. Large exhibition at the Galerie Georges Petit, Paris, comprising 225 paintings, 7 sculptures and 6 illustrated books. Special number of the review "Cahiers d'Art" on Picasso.

1935

Wrote poetry and engraved the "Minotauromachy". Birth of a daughter Maia. Jaime Sabartès became his secretary.

1936

Itinerant exhibition of his works shown at Barcelona, Bilbao and Madrid; preface to the catalogue by Paul Eluard. Outbreak of the Spanish Civil War and Picasso, who supported the Republican side, was appointed Director of the Prado.

1937

Illustrated the "Sueño y Mentira de Franco" (Franco's Dream and Lie) with engravings and painted *Guernica* for the Spanish Pavilion at the Exposition Universelle in Paris.

1939-1944

Large retrospective exhibition at the Museum of Modern Art, New York.

War declared when Picasso was at Antibes. After spending a year at Royan, he returned to Paris where he stayed for the rest of the occupation. In 1941, wrote a short play, "le Désir attrapé par la queue", performed at the home of Michel and Louise Leiris by amateur actors, who included Sartre and Camus. After the liberation of Paris in 1944, he exhibited at the Salon d'Automne with 74 paintings and 5 sculptures. Joined the Communist Party the same year.

1946

Picasso spent most of the year on the French Riviera with Françoise Gilot. The Curator of the Antibes Museum put the Palais Grimaldi at his disposition, where he worked for four months. Left serie of *Antipolis* on loan there, which he had painted during this period.

1947-1949
Stayed several times in the south of France, especially at Vallauris, where he settled and revived the art of pottery. Performance of Alain Resnais's film *Guernica* with a commentary by Paul Eluard.

1951
Several exhibitions of his work notably at Tokyo and London to celebrate Picasso's seventieth birthday.

1952
Painted two large panels, *War* and *Peace*, later placed in a disused chapel at Vallauris.

1953
Several exhibitions at Lyon, Rome, Milan and São Paulo.

1954
Françoise Gilot left Picasso and he married Jacqueline Roque. During a stay in Paris, painted a series of fifteen variations on Delacroix's *Femmes d'Alger*. Exhibition during the summer at the Maison de la Pensée Française, including notably thirty-seven paintings loaned by the U.S.S.R. from Shchukin's former collection.

1955
Retrospective exhibition at the Louvre and the Bibliothèque Nationale, Paris. Same exhibition shown at London the following year. Moved into the villa "La Californie", Cannes, and worked with Clouzot on his film "Mystère de Picasso".

1957
Began a series of fifty-seven variations on Velazquez's *Las Meninas*, which were exhibited at the Galerie Louise Leiris, Paris, in 1959. Large retrospective organized by Alfred Barr and held first at the Museum of Modern Art, New York, then at Philadelphia and Chicago.

1958
Large mural for the UNESCO building in Paris. Bought the Château de Vauvenargues, near Aix-en-Provence.

1960
Large retrospective at the Tate Gallery, London.

1961
Series of 150 drawings and 27 paintings after Manet's *Déjeuner sur l'herbe*, which were exhibited at the Galerie Louise Leiris, Paris.

1963
Painted a number of large pictures on the theme of the Painter and his Model, or the Painter at his Easel.

Picasso Museum opened at Barcelona.

1964-1965
Large exhibitions at Montreal, Toronto, and Tokyo.

1966
Vast retrospective to celebrate Picasso's eighty-fifth birthday in Paris at the museums of the Grand and Petit Palais and the Bibliothèque Nationale.

1968
Exhibition of a large group of engravings at the Galerie Louise Leiris, Paris. Picasso donated the complete series of *Las Meninas* to the Picasso Museum, Barcelona, in memory of the his friend Jaime Sabartès.

1970-1971
Exhibition at the Palais des Papes in Avignon. Second donation to the Picasso. Museum at Barcelona. Exhibition of drawings and pastels at the Galerie Louise Leiris.

1972
Exhibition of 172 drawings at the Galerie Louise Leiris.

1973
January: Exhibition of 156 engravings at the Galerie Louise Leiris in Paris. April 8: Picasso died at Mougins. Buried at Vauvenargues.

LIST OF PLATES

PLANCHES

PLATES

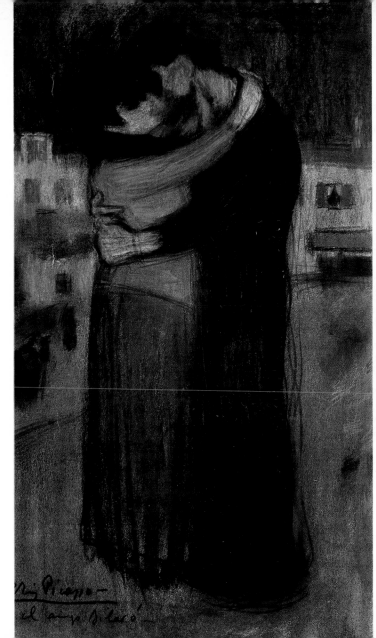

1
Les Amants
dans la rue
1900
Lovers in the
Street

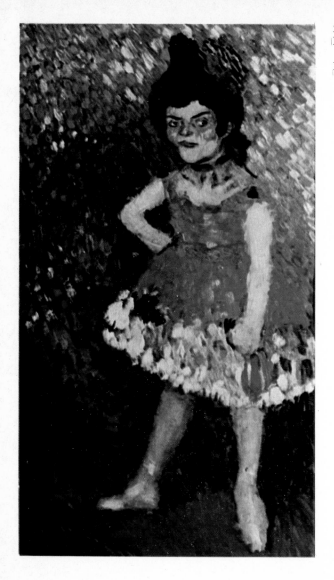

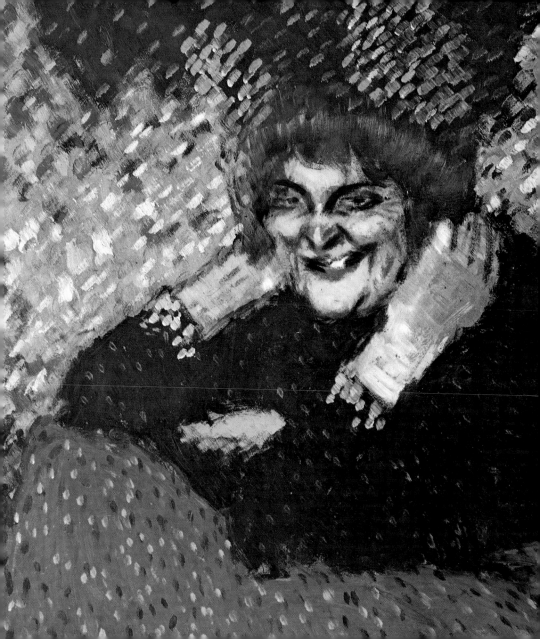

4 Corrida 1901

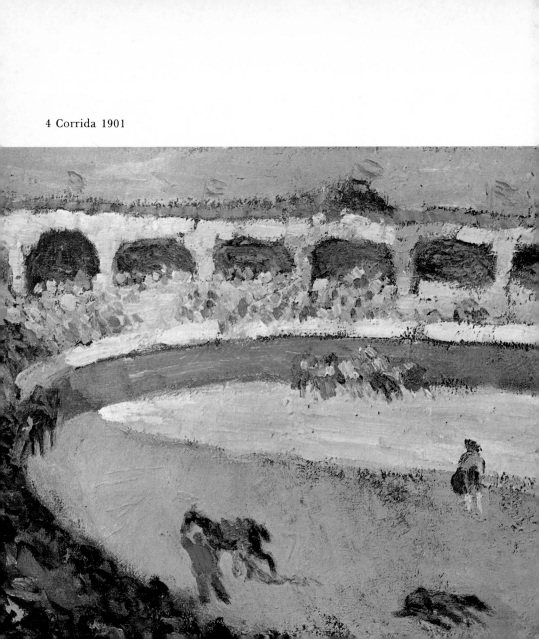

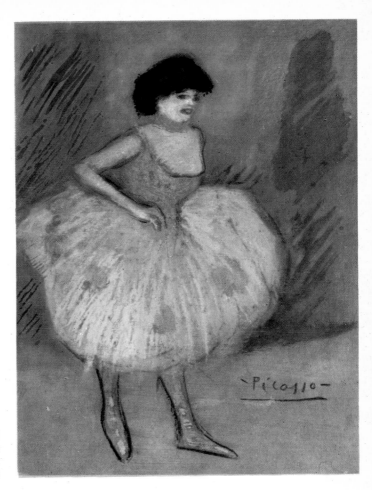

5
Ballerine
1901
Ballerina

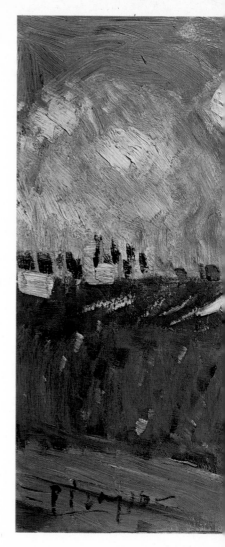

6
Les Toits bleus
1901
The Blue Roofs

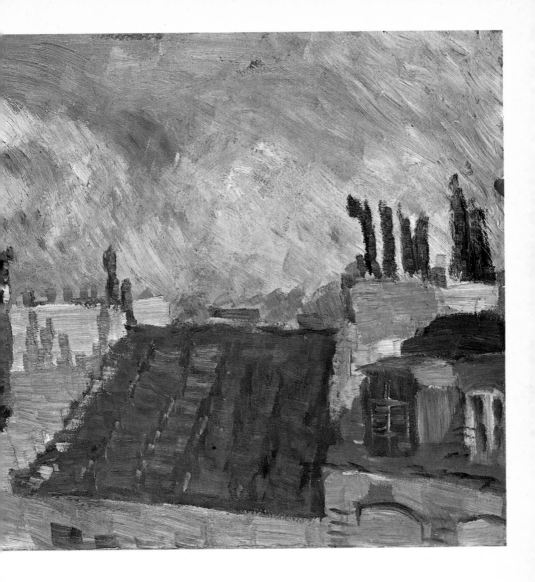

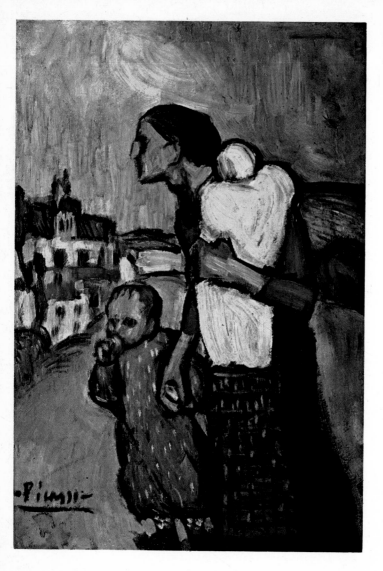

7
La Mère
1901
The Mother

8
Deux femmes
assises au bar
1901
Women at a Bar

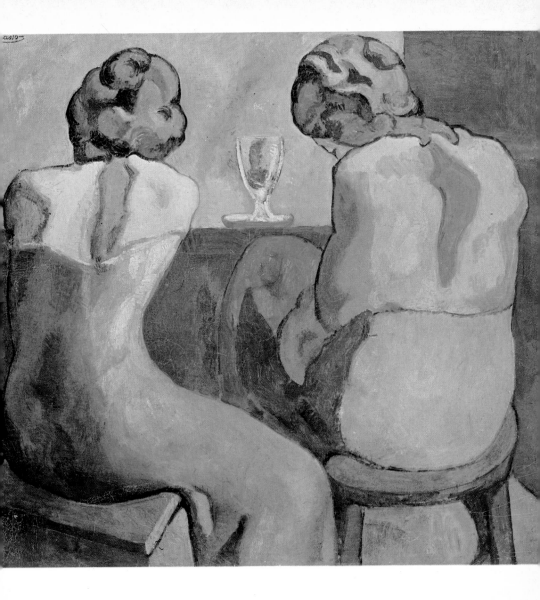

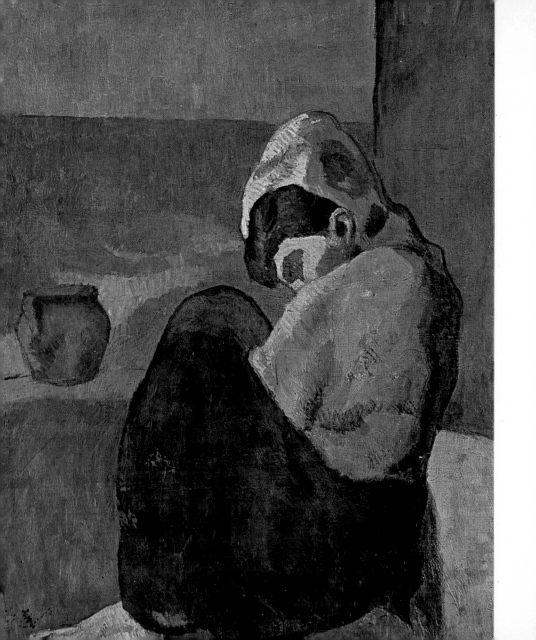

9
Femme assise
avec capuchon
1902
Seated Woman
with a Hood

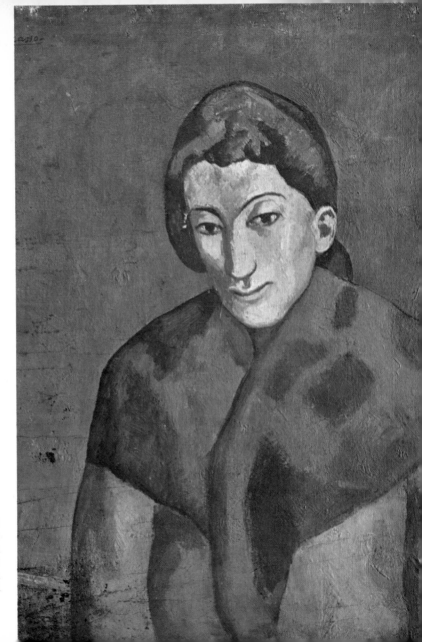

10
Femme au
fichu bleu
1902
Woman with
a blue Shawl

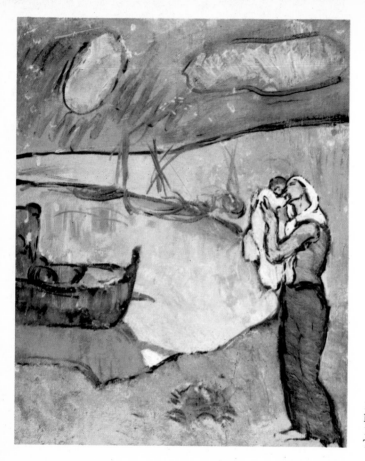

11
Les Adieux du pêcheur
1902
The Fisherman's Farewell

12
L'Étreinte
1903
The Embrace

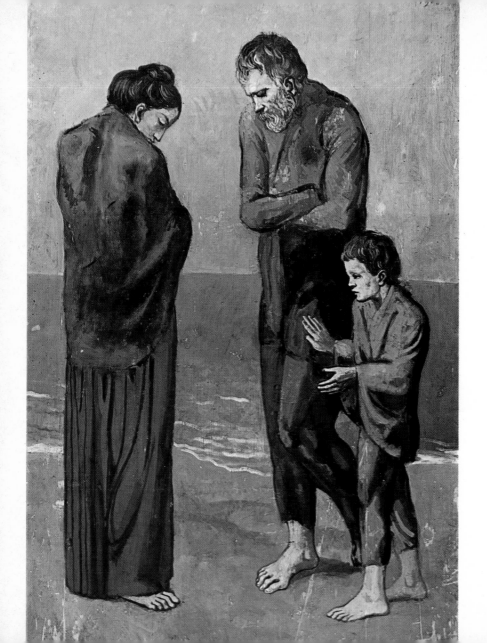

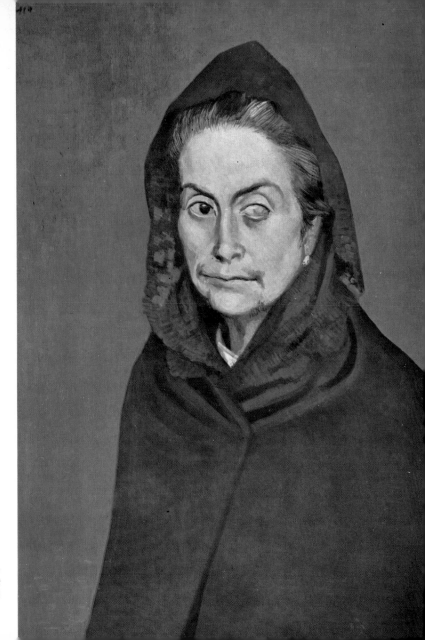

13
Les Pauvres
au bord de la mer
1903
Poor Folk by
the Sea

14
La Célestine
1903

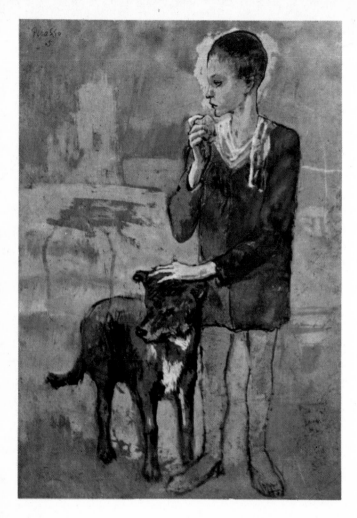

15
L'Enfant au chien
1905
Child with a Dog

16
Nu assis
1905
Seated Nude

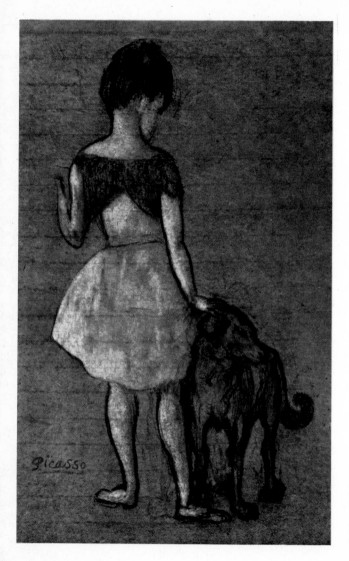

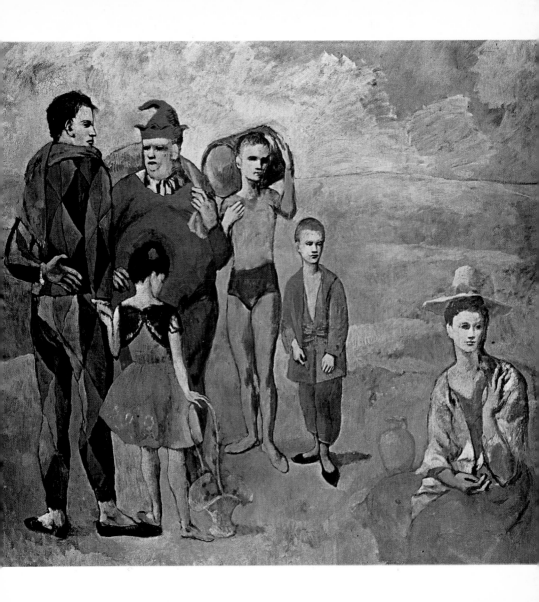

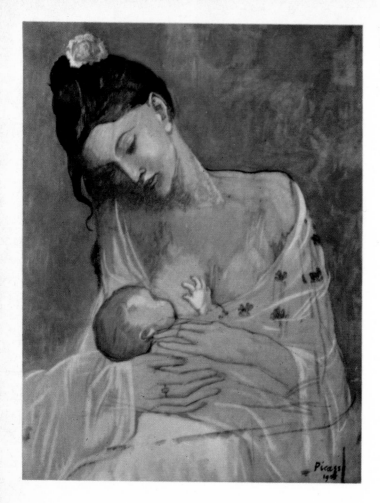

19
Maternité
1905
Maternity

20
Femme à l'éventail
1905
Girl with a Fan

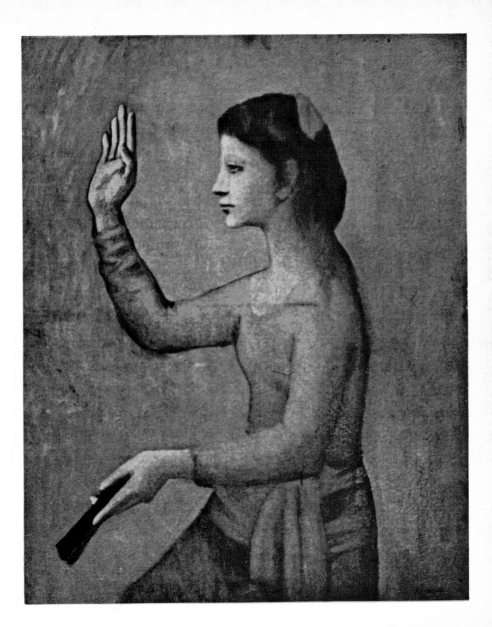

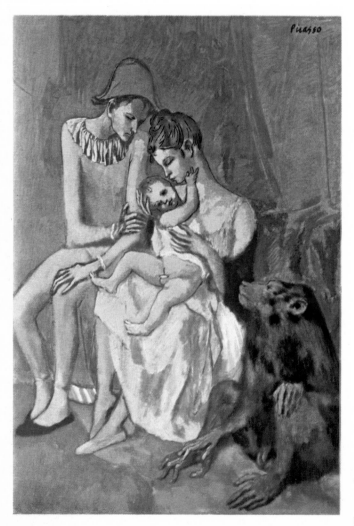

21
Famille d'acrobates
avec singe
1905
Family of Acrobats
with a Monkey

22
Jeune écuyère
1905
Young Rider

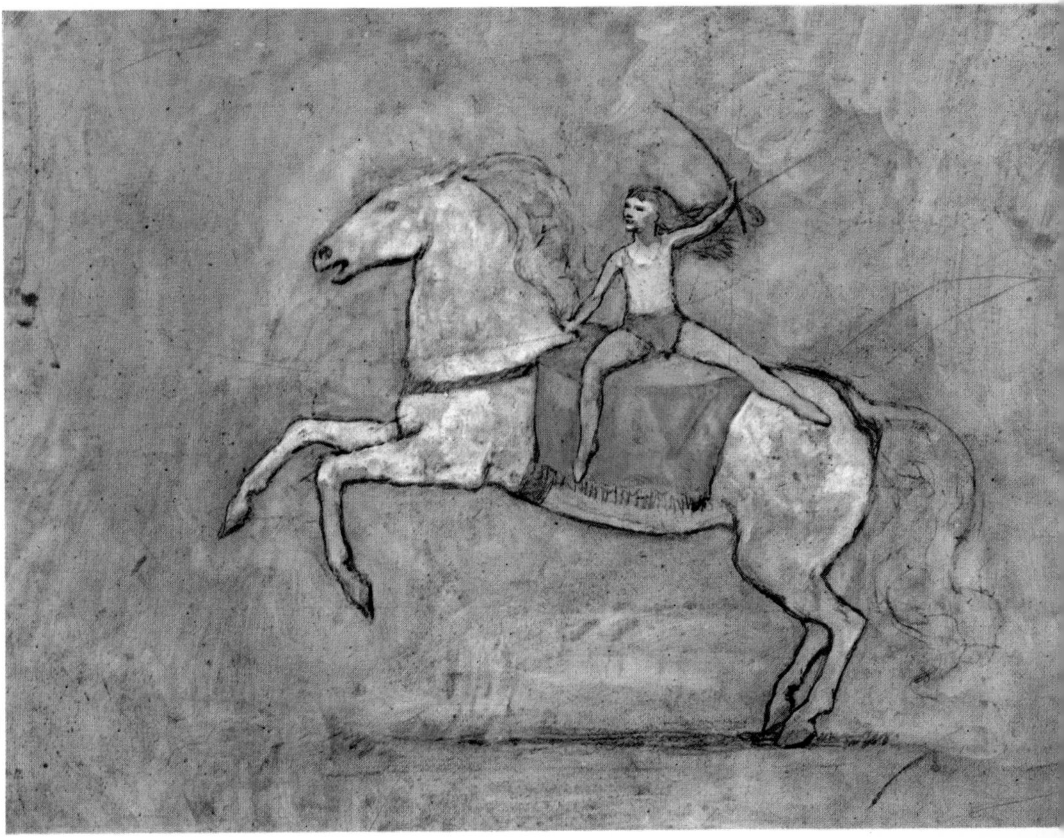

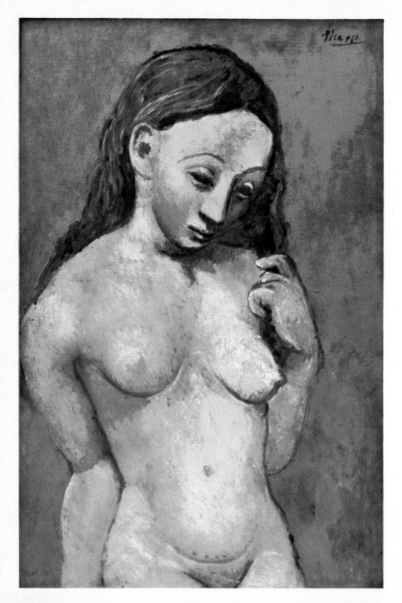

23
Nu sur
fond rouge
1906
Nude against
a Red Background

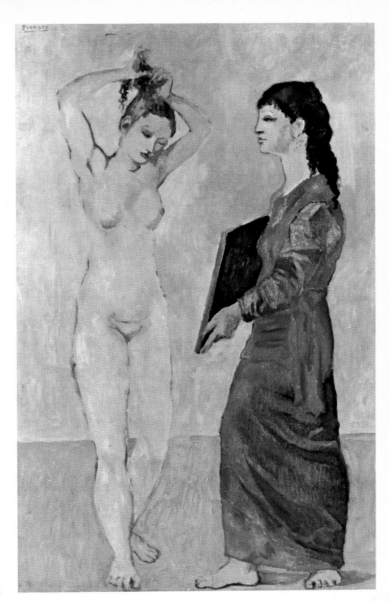

24
La Toilette
1906
The Toilet

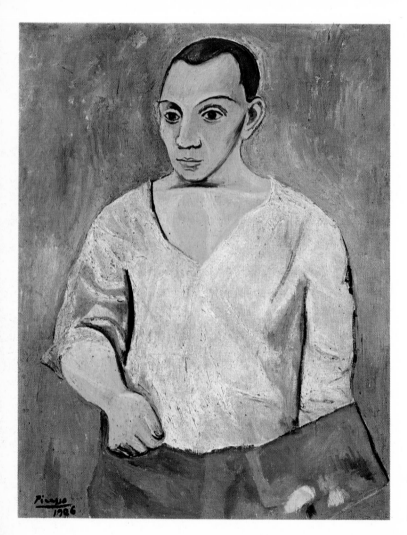

26
Gertrude Stein
1906

25
Autoportrait
à la palette
1906
Self-Portrait

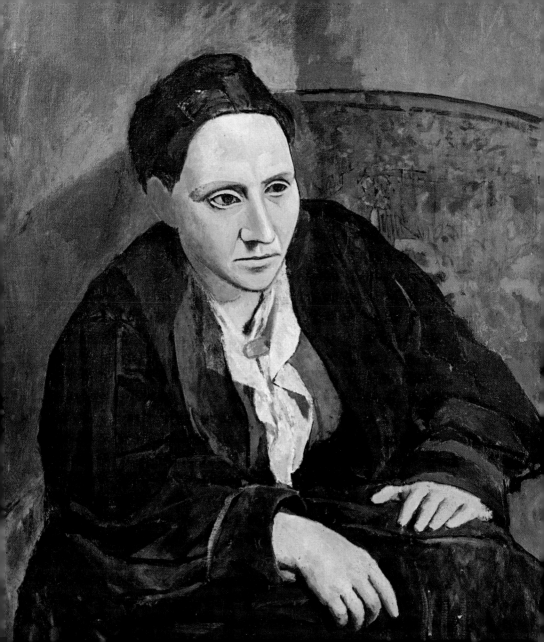

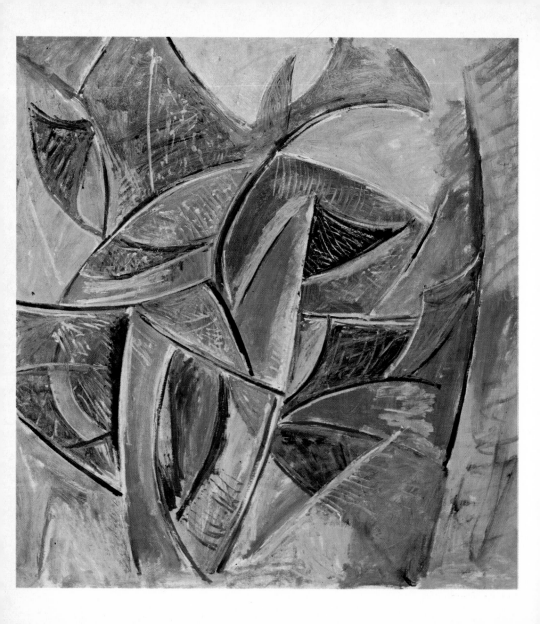

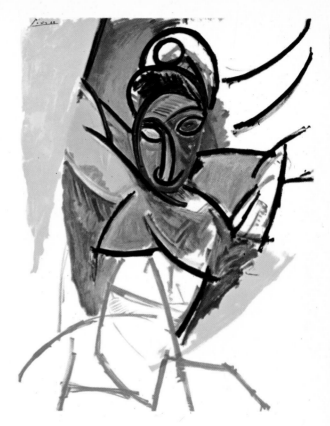

28 Étude pour Les Demoiselles d'Avignon.
   1907. Study for « Les Demoiselles d'Avignon ».

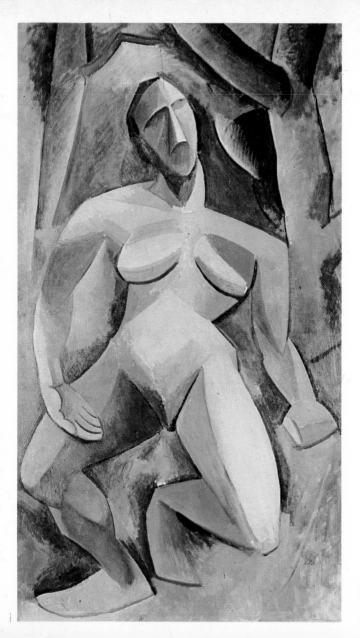

30
Les Demoiselles
d'Avignon
1907

29
Nu dans la forêt
1908
Nude in a Forest

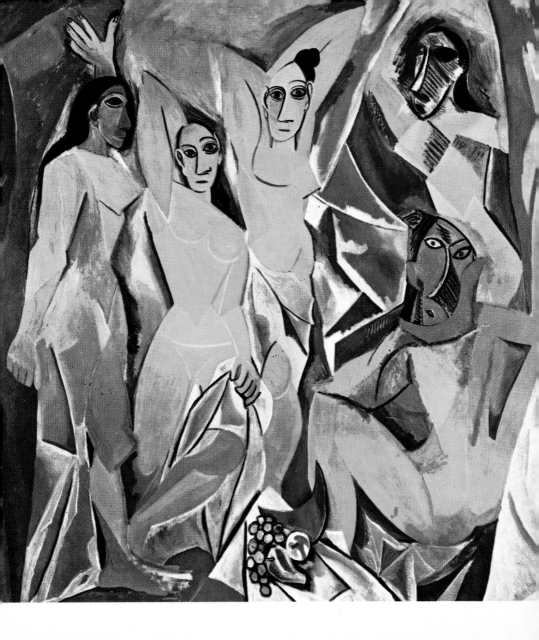

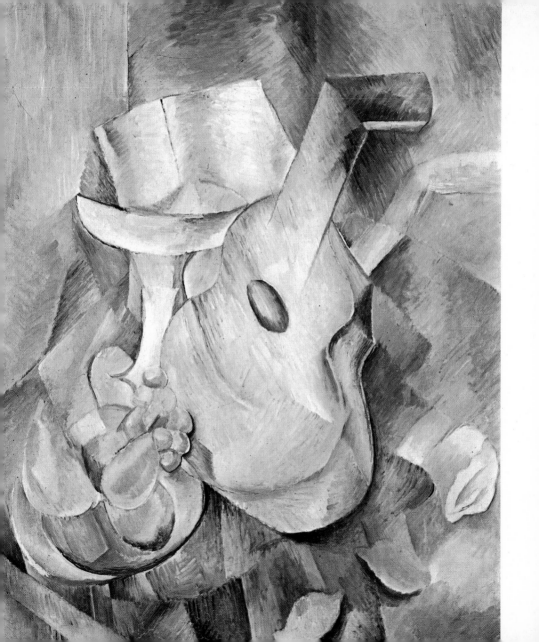

31
Compotier aux poires
1909
Fruit-Dish with Pears

32 Usine à Horta de Ebro. 1909. The Factory.

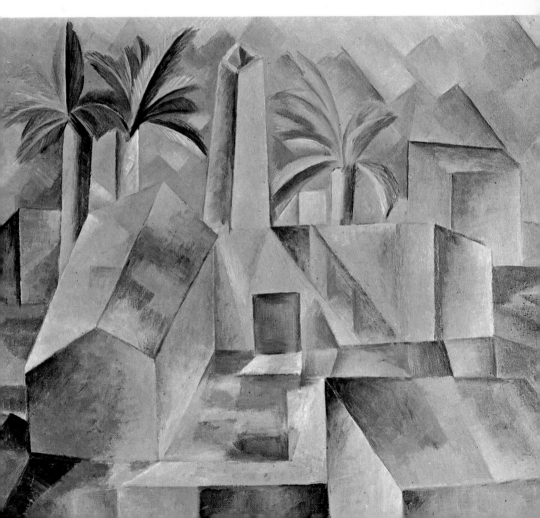

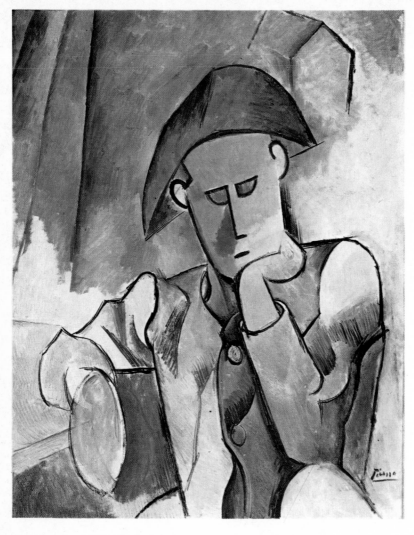

33 Arlequin. 1909. Harlequin.

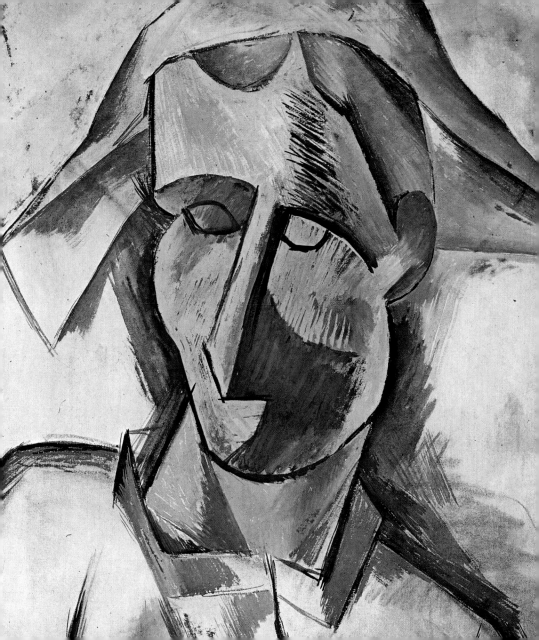

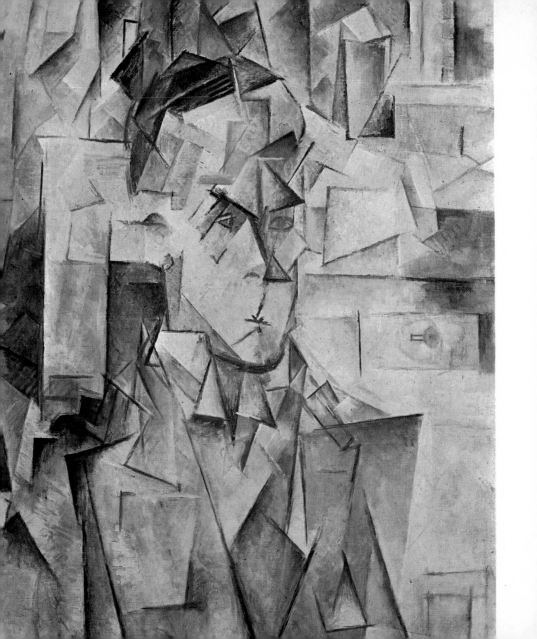

35
Wilhelm Uhde
1910

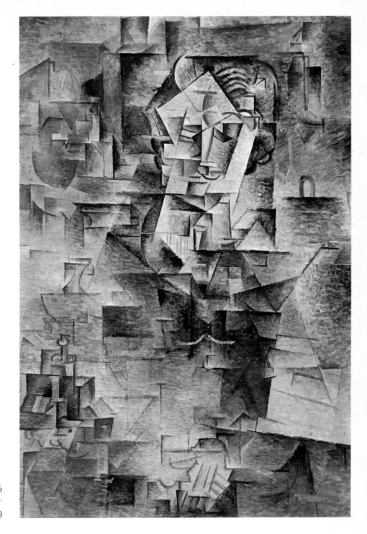

36
D.H. Kahnweiler
1910

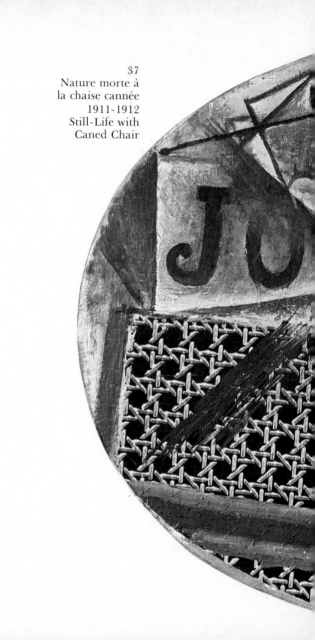

37
Nature morte à
la chaise cannée
1911-1912
Still-Life with
Caned Chair

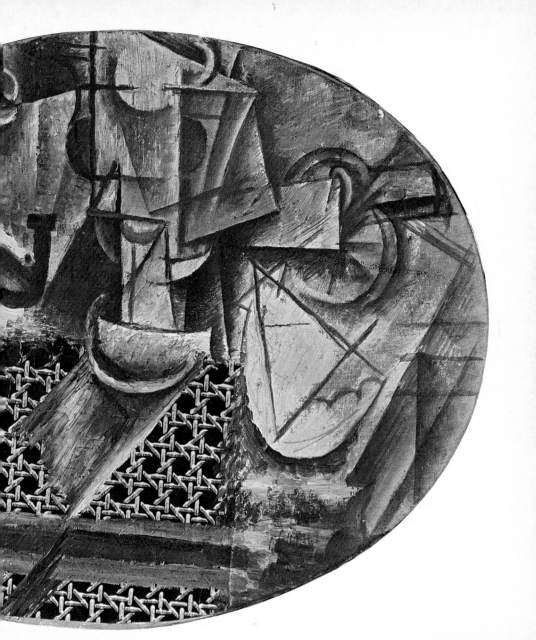

38 Bouteille, verre et violon
1912. Bottle, Wine-Glass and Violin

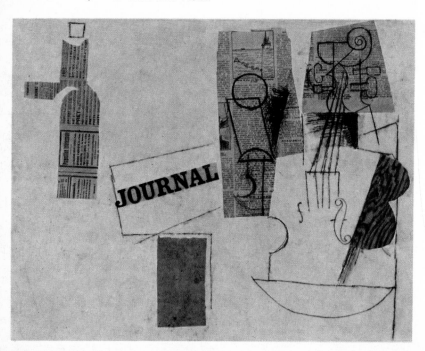

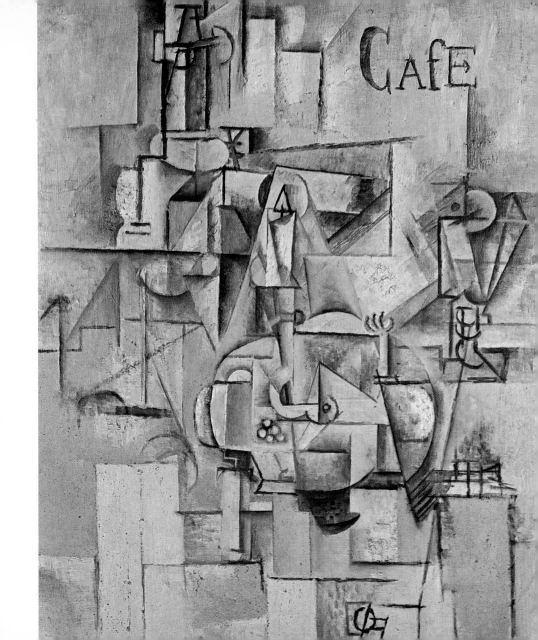

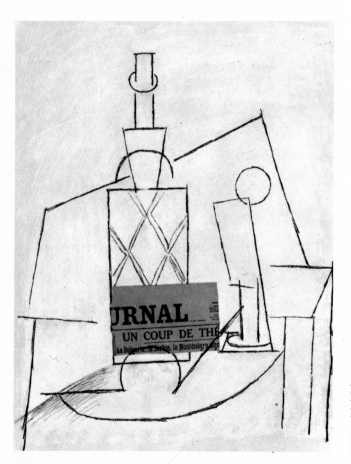

40
Bouteille de rhum
paillée et verre
1912
Glass with Straw-Bound
Bottle of Rum

41
L'Aficionado
1912
'he Aficionado

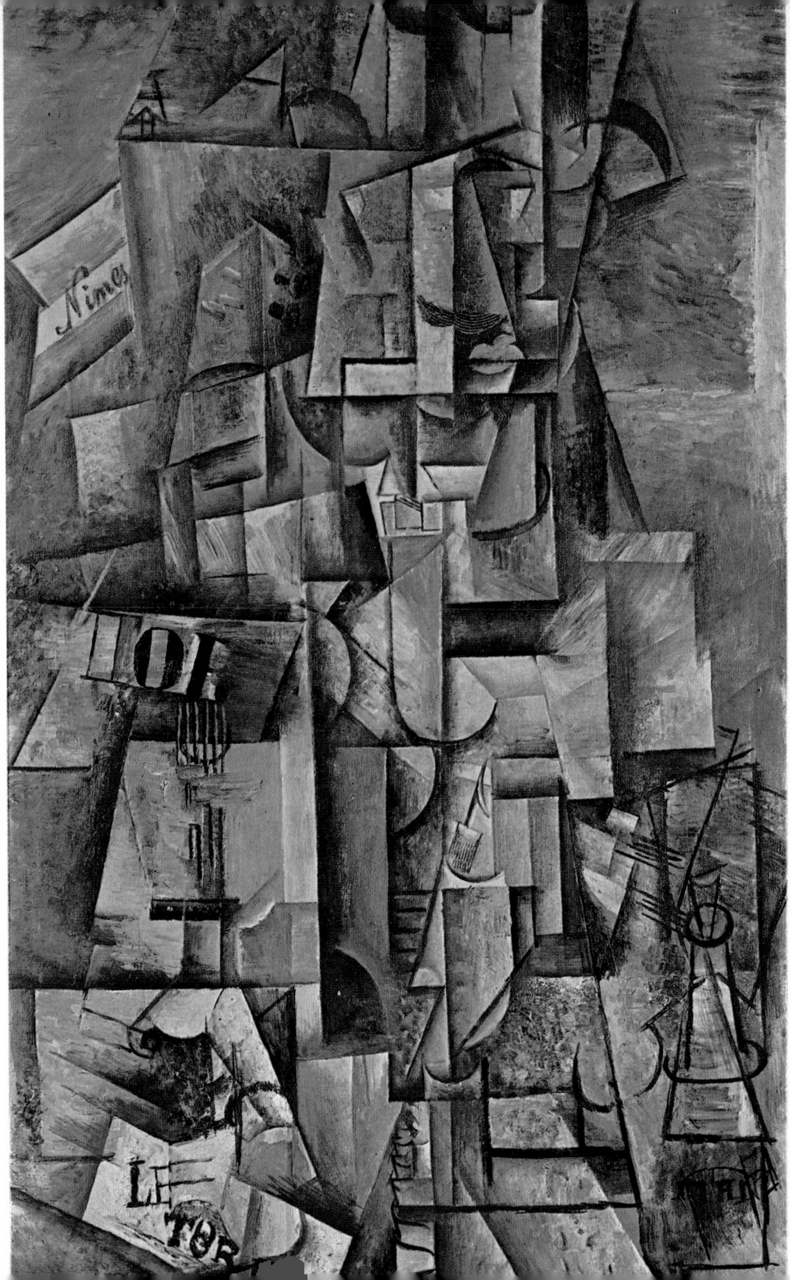

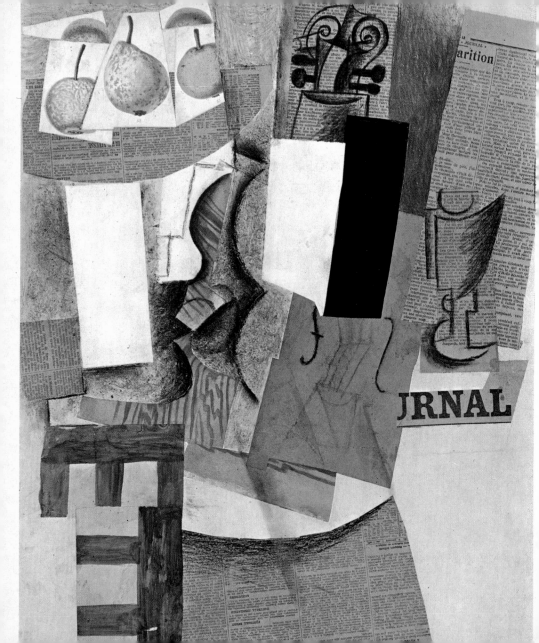

42
Nature morte :
violon et fruits
1912-1913
Still-Life with
Violin and Fruits

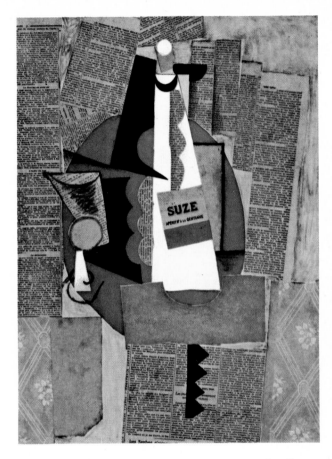

43 Bouteille de Suze. 1912-1913. Bottle of Suze.

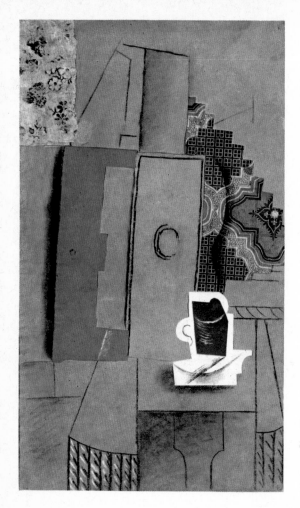

44
Guitare
et tasse de café
1913
Guitar and
Coffe Cup

45
Bouteille de Bass
1912
Bottle of Bass

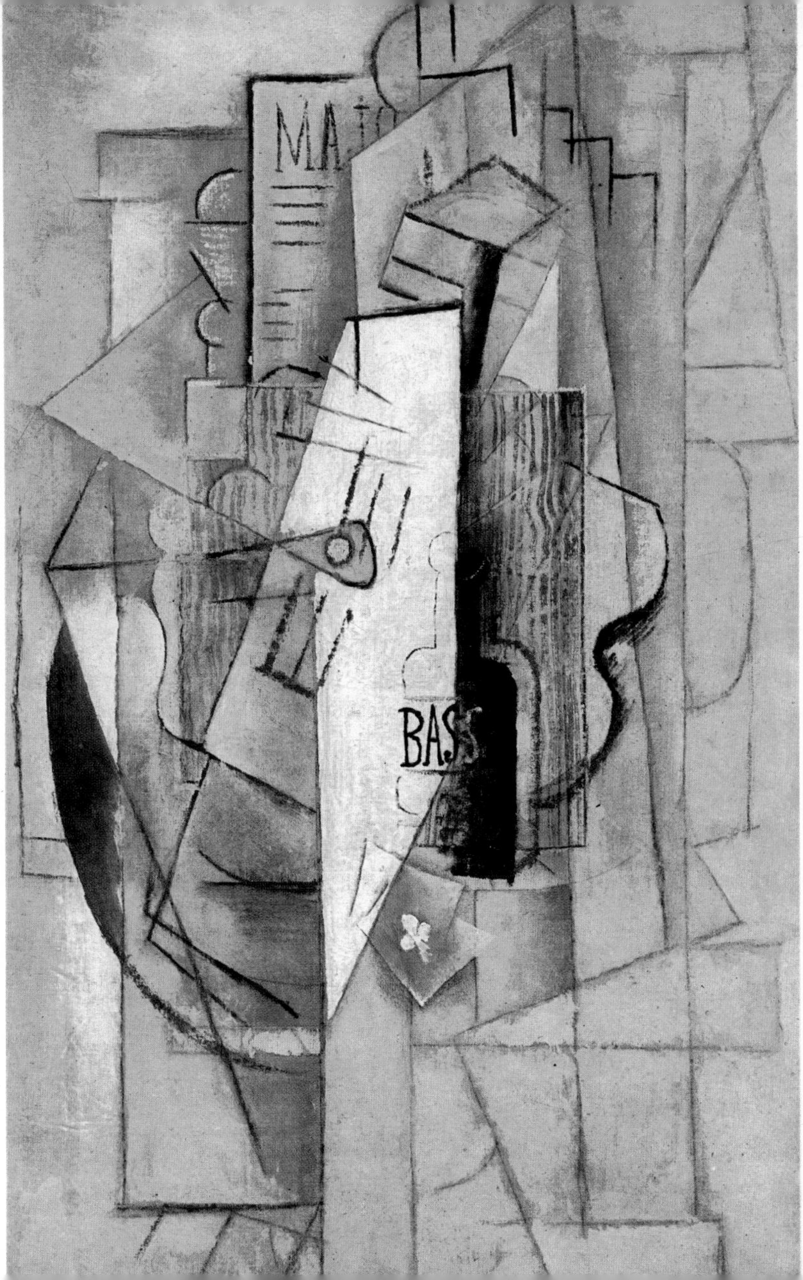

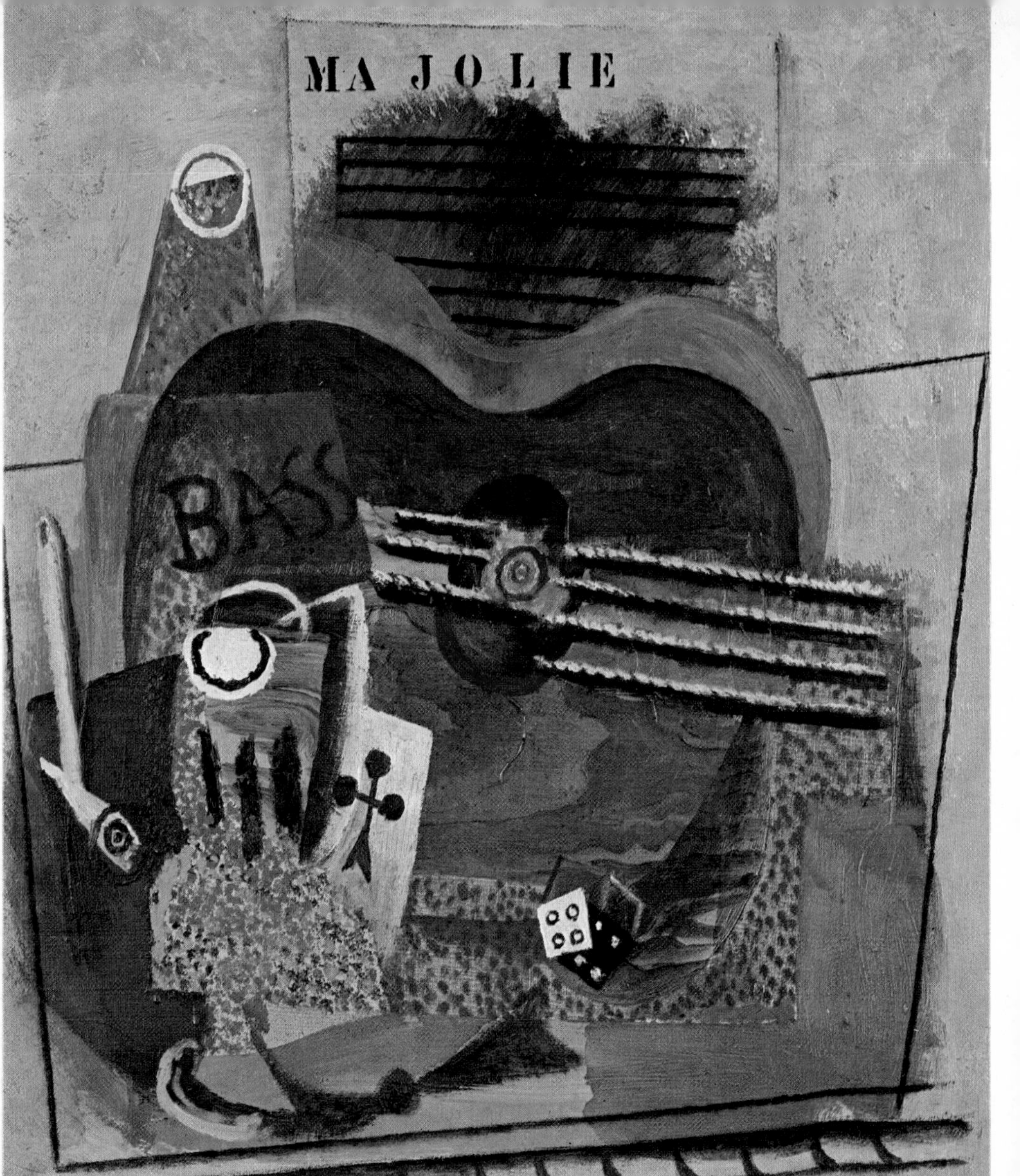
MA JOLIE
BASS

46
Ma Jolie : pipe,
verre et carte à jouer
1914
« Ma Jolie » : Pipe, Glass
and Playing-Card

47 Bouteille de Bass, verre, paquet de tabac et carte de visite
1913-19. Bottle of Bass, Glass, Packet of Tobacco and Visiting-Card

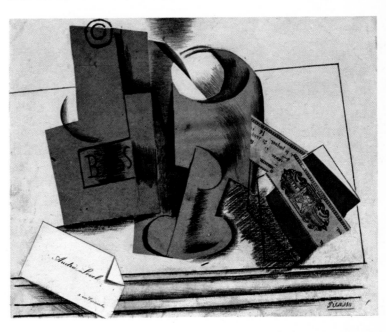

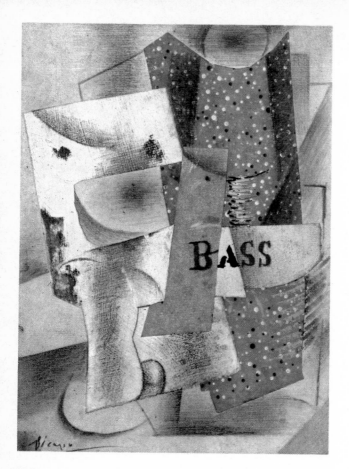

48 Nature morte avec « Bass »
1914 Still-Life with « Bass »

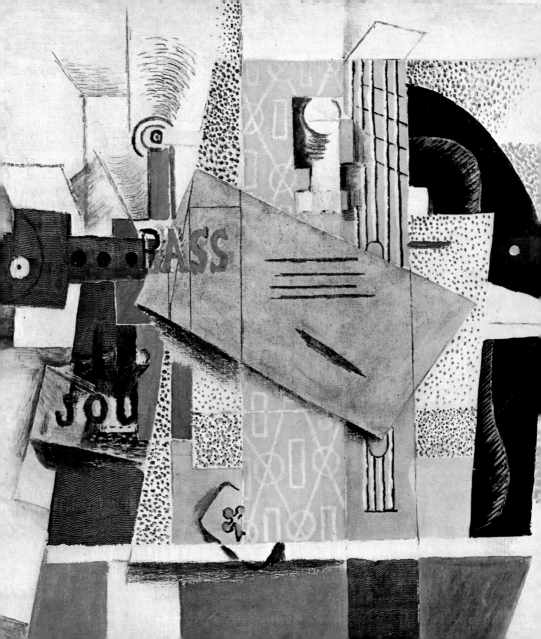

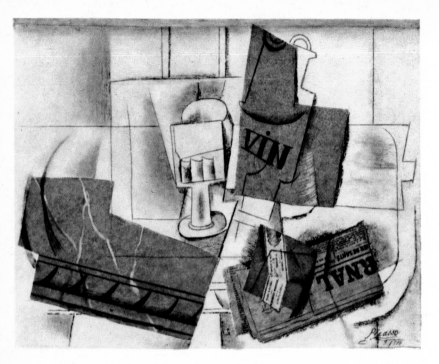

50 Verre, paquet de tabac et journal sur une table
1914 Still-Life with Newspaper and Pack of Tobacco

51
Portrait de jeune fille
1914
Portrait of a Girl against
a Green Background

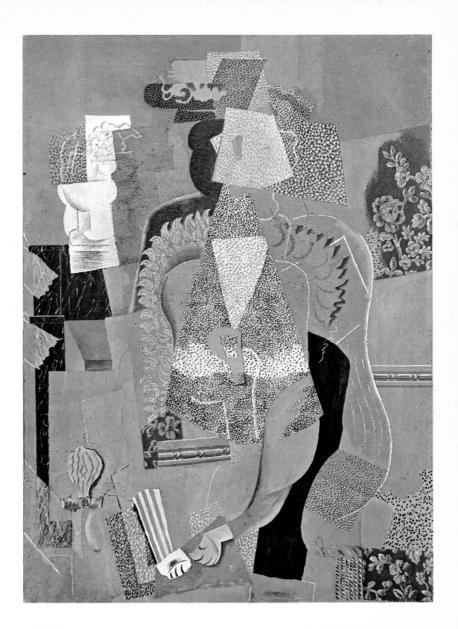

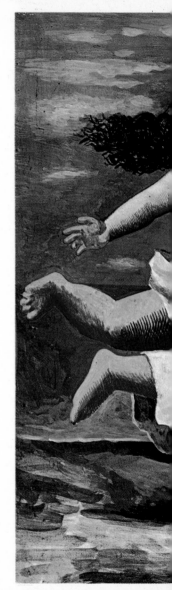

52
Deux Femmes
courant
sur la plage
1922
The Race

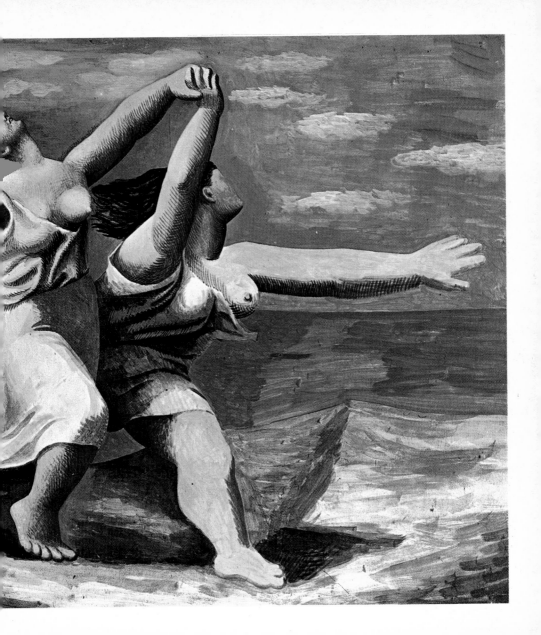

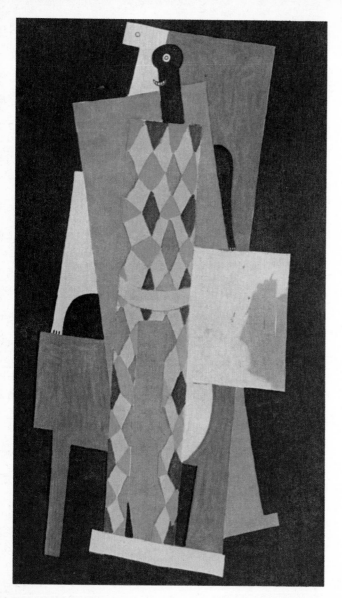

53
Arlequin
1915
Harlequin

54
Pierrot assis
1918
Seated Pierrot

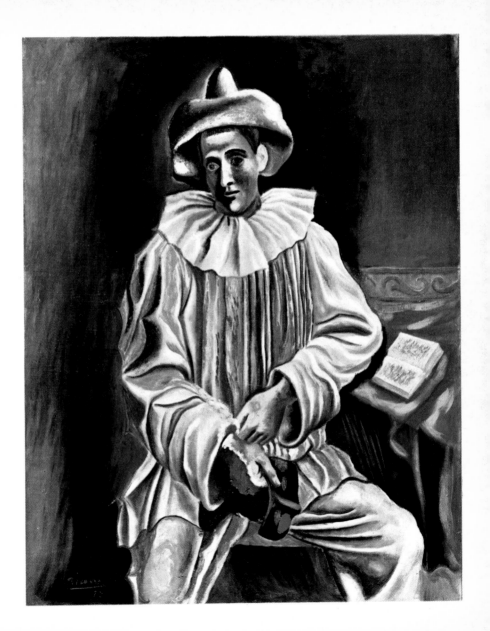

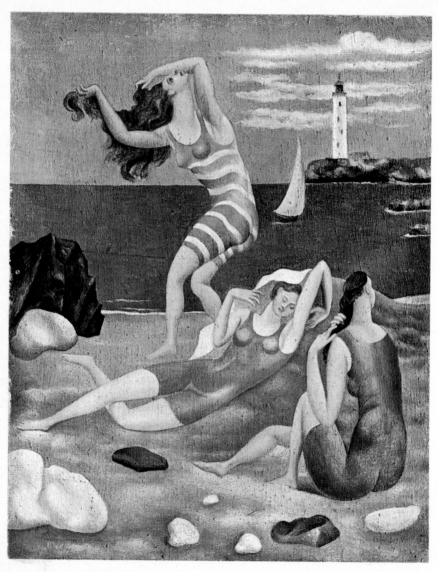

55
Baigneuses
1918
Bathers

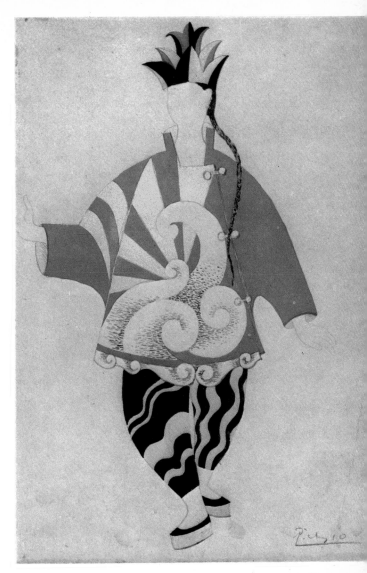

56
Costume
pour Parade
Étude pour le
prestidigitateur
chinois
1917
Costume for
Parade. Study
for the Chinese
Conjuror

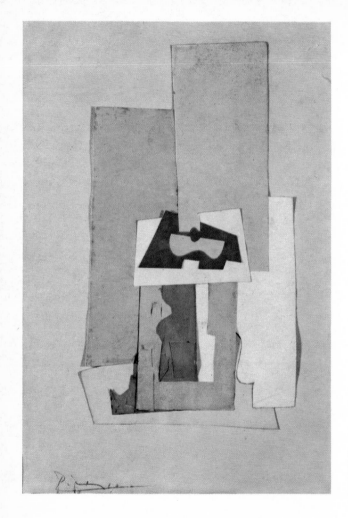

57
Guitare sur un guéridon
1919
Guitar on a Table

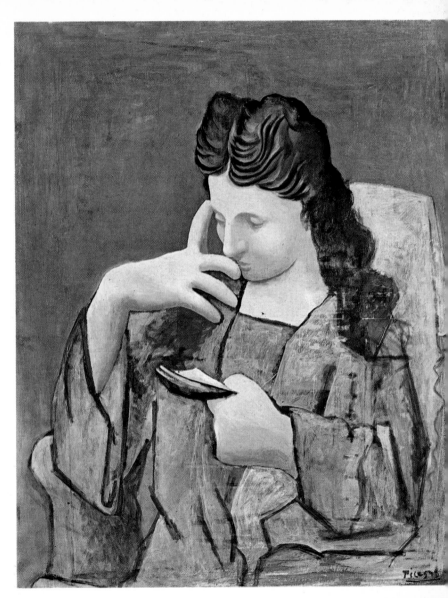

59 Femme au voile bleu. 1923. Woman with a Blue Veil.

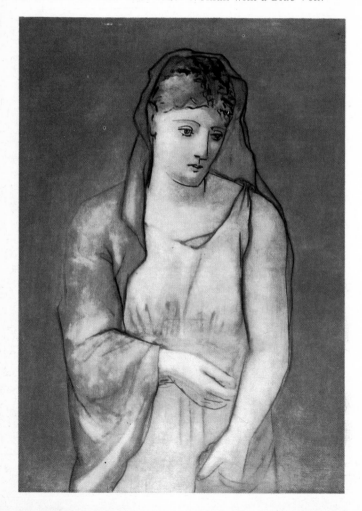

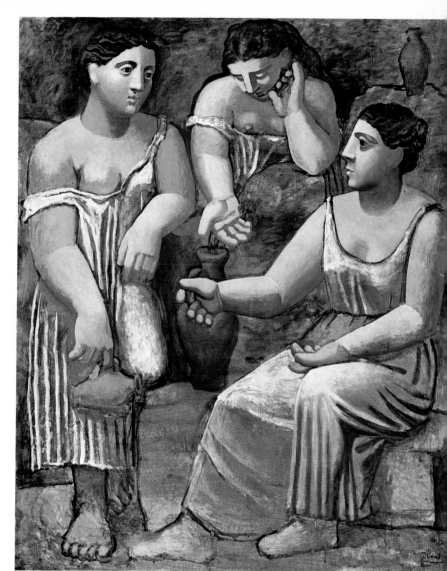

60
Trois Femmes
à la fontaine
1921
Three Women at
the Fountain

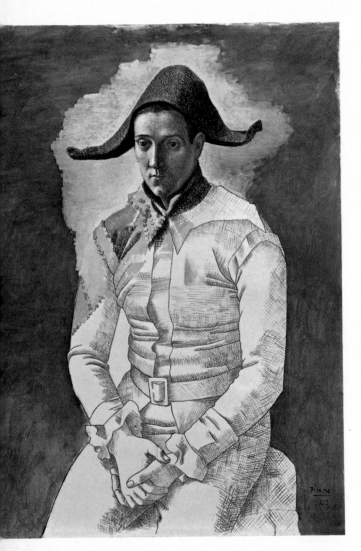

61
Arlequin
1923
Harlequin

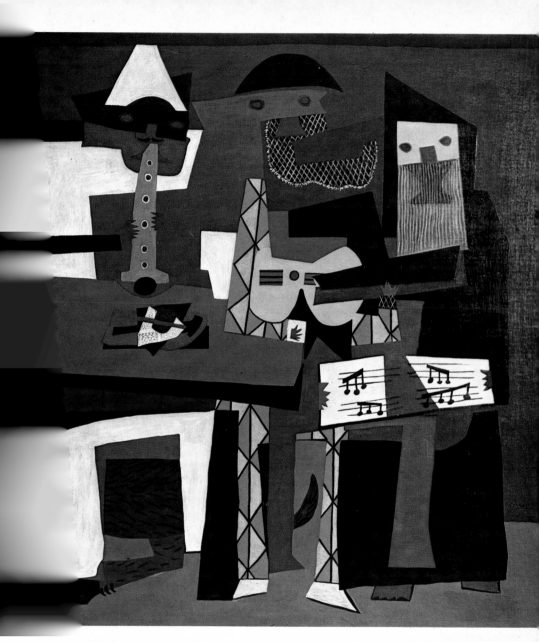

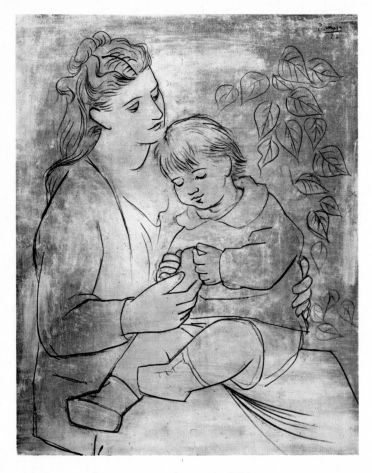

63 Mère et Enfant. 1922. Mother and Child.

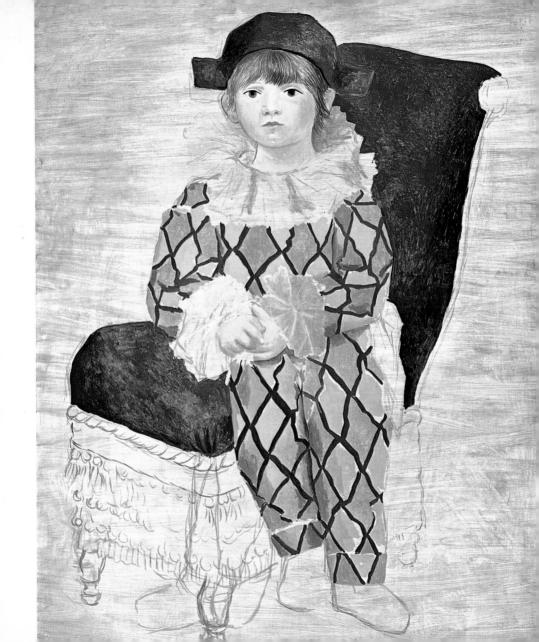

65 Nature morte au buste et à la palette
1925. Still-Life with Bust and Palette

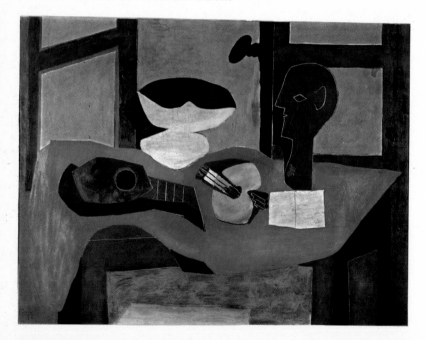

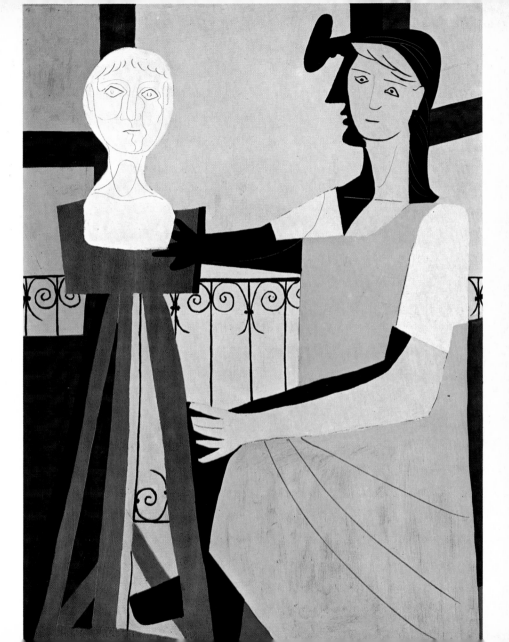

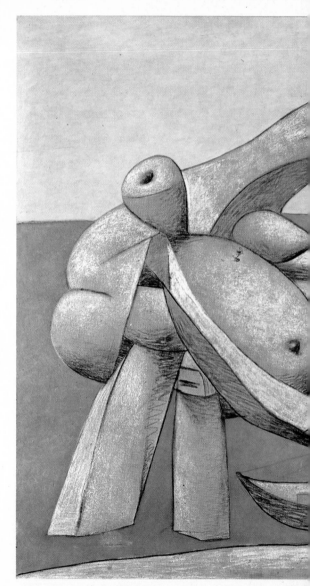

67
Femmes sur la plage
1937
Women on the Beach

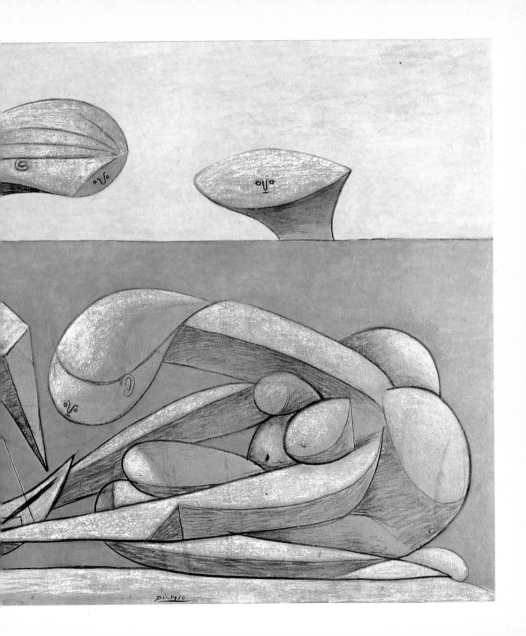

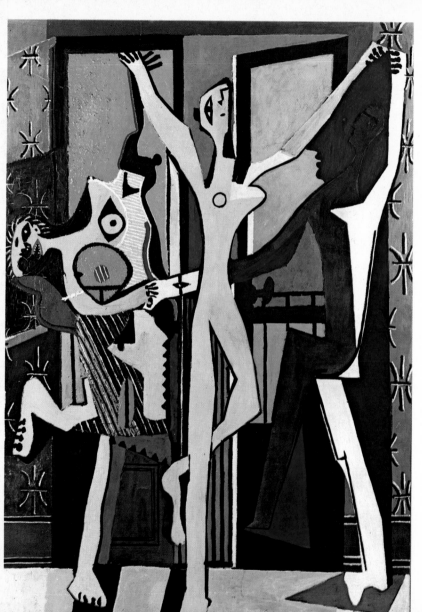

68
La Danse
1925
Three Dancers

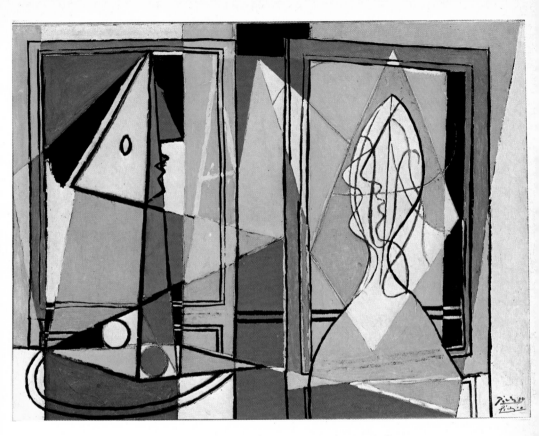

69 Deux Femmes à la fenêtre. 1927. Two Women by a Window.

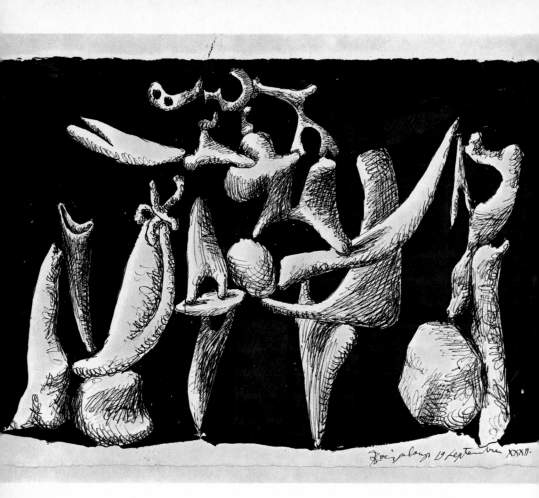

70 Crucifixion 1932

71
Nature morte
sur un guéridon
1931
Still-Life
on a Table

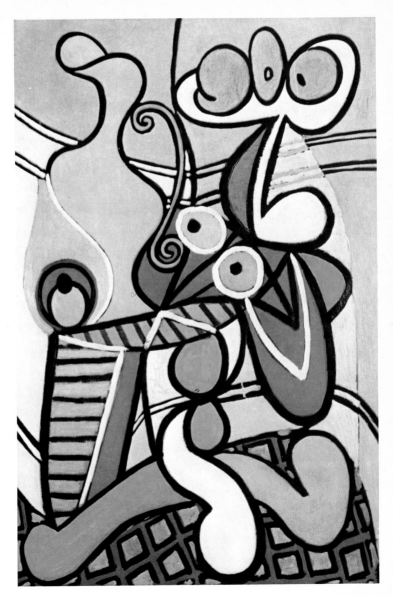

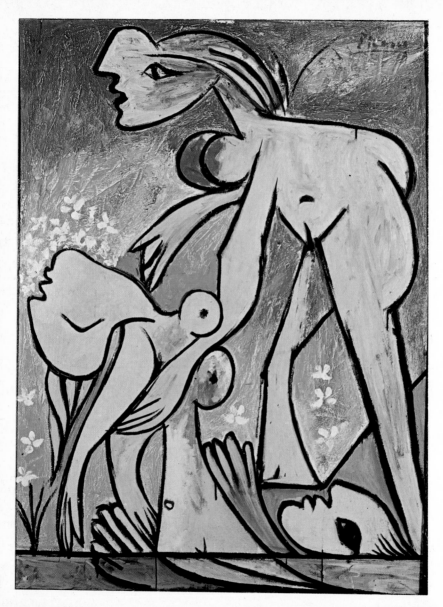

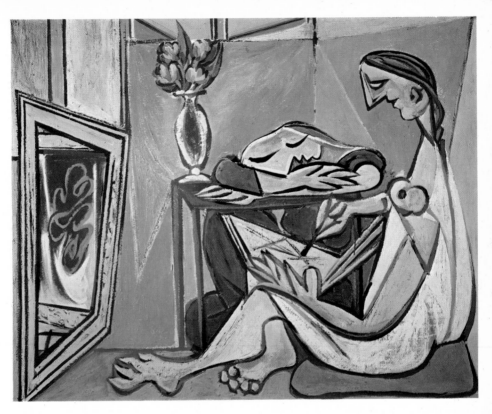

73 La Muse. 1935. The Muse.

74 Tête de cheval. 1937. Horse's Head.

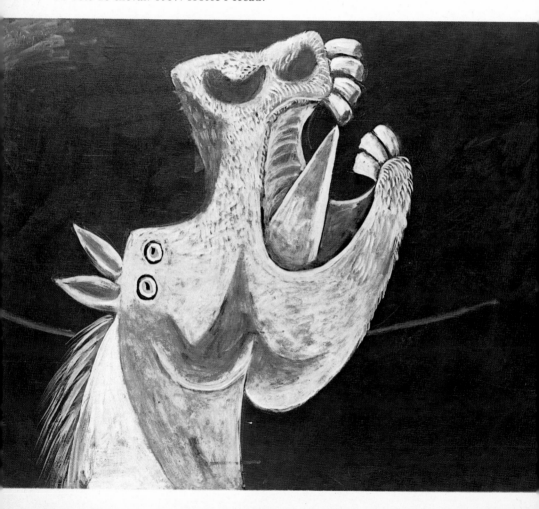

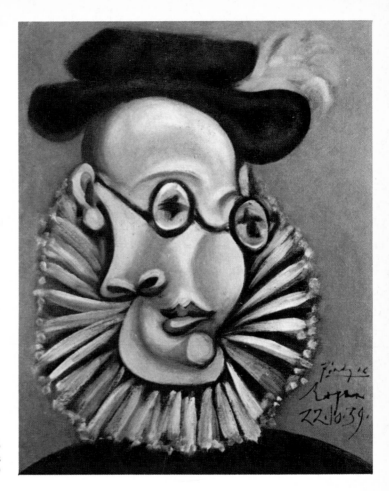

75
Jaime Sabartès
1939

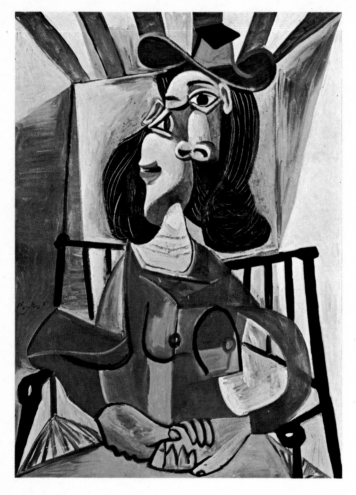

76 Femme assise dans un fauteuil
   1941. Woman Seated in an Armchair

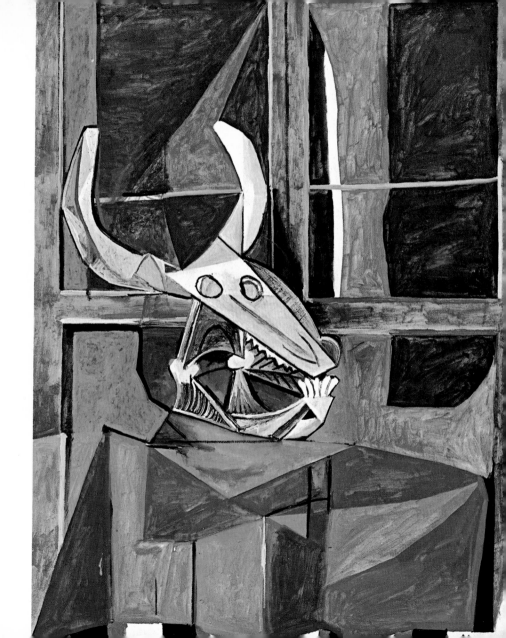

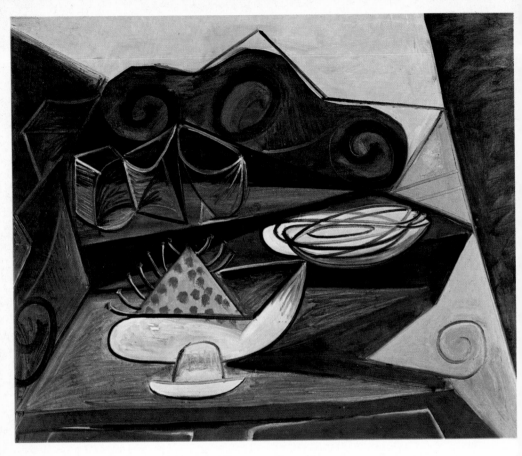

78 Le Buffet du Catalan. 1943. The Buffet at the « Catalan ».

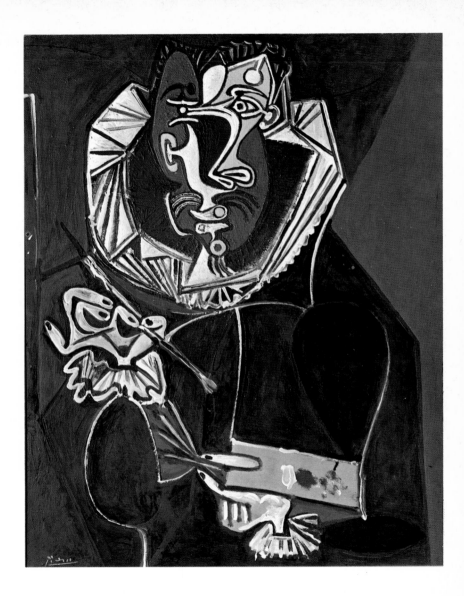

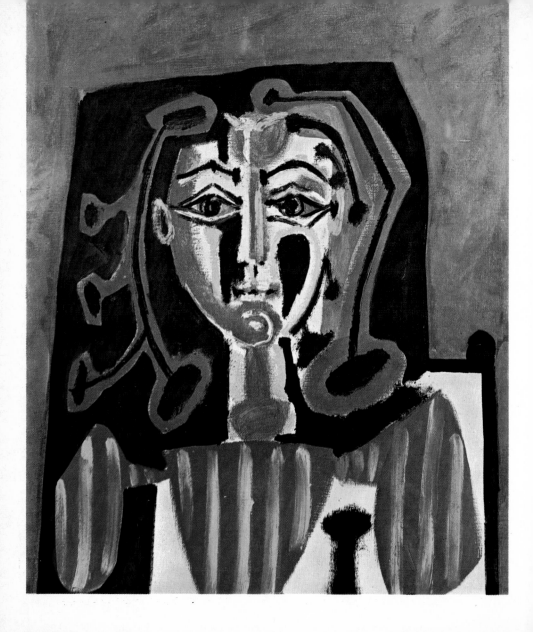

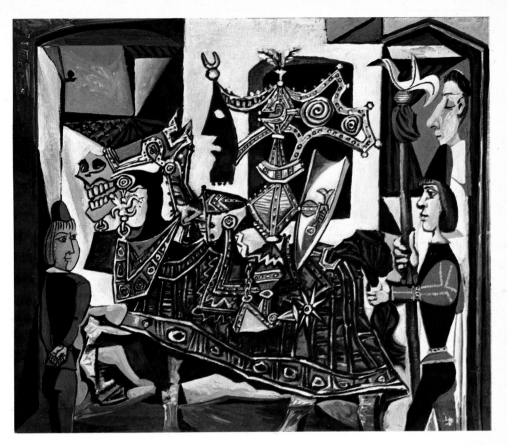

81 Jeu de pages 1951

80
Portrait de
jeune fille
1949
Portrait of
a Young Girl

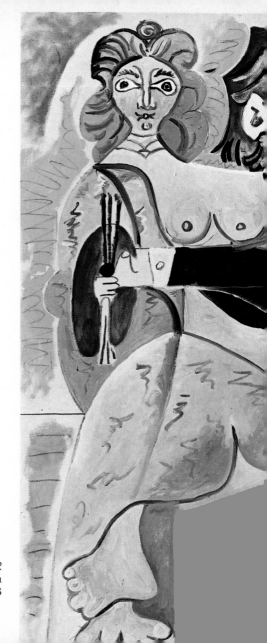

82
Rembrandt et Saskia
1963

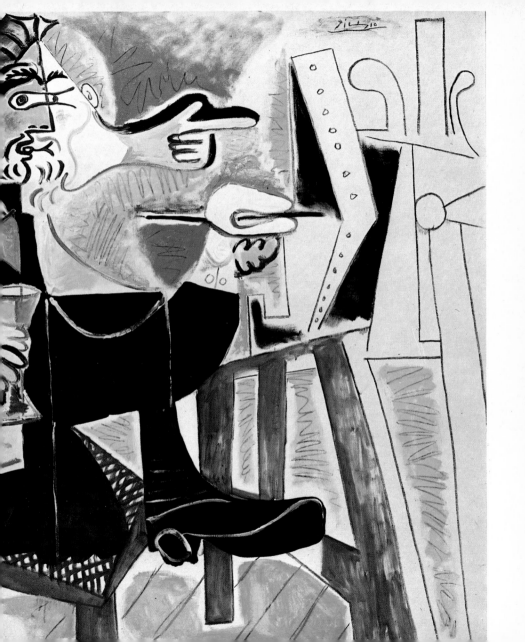

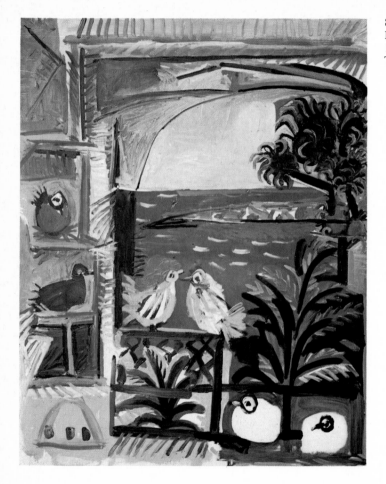

83
Les Pigeons
1957
The Pigeons

84
Les Femmes d'Alger
1955
Women of Algiers

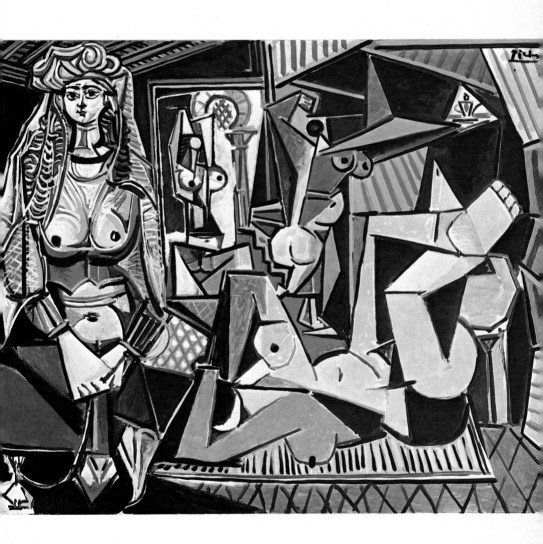

85 Nu dans un jardin. 1956. Nude in a Garden.

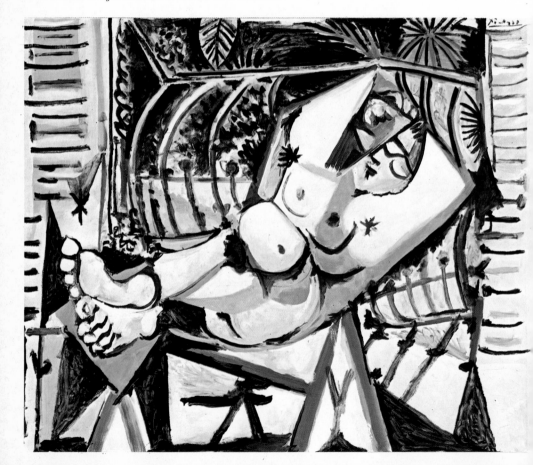

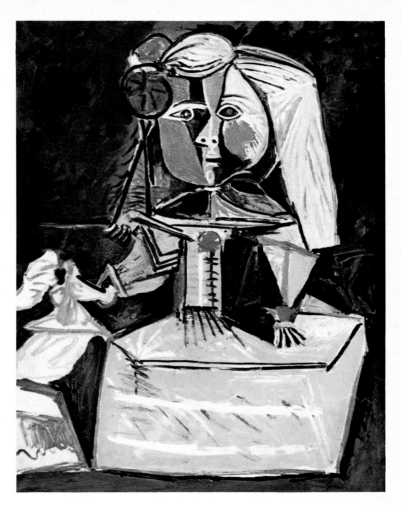

86
Les Ménines
1957
Las Meninas

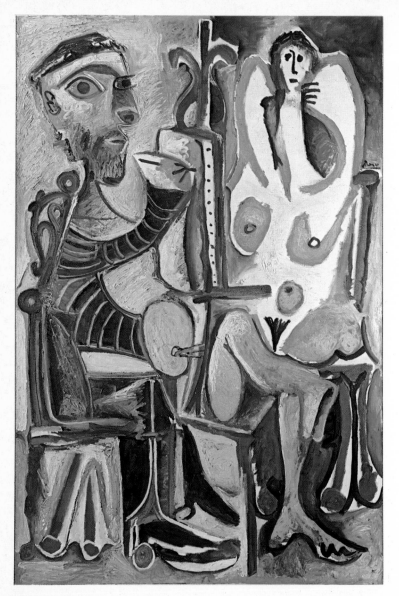

87
Le Peintre
et son Modèle
1963
The Painter
and his Model

88 Le Peintre et son Modèle. 1963. The Painter and his Model.

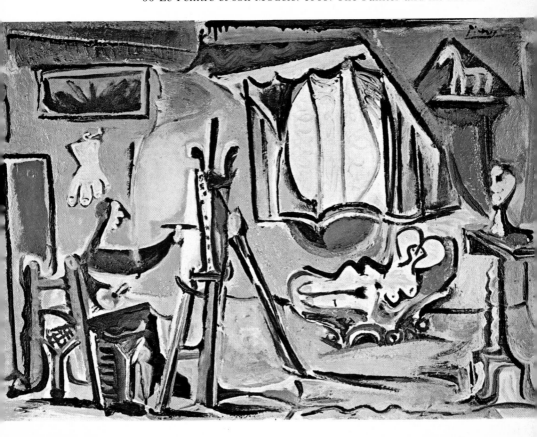

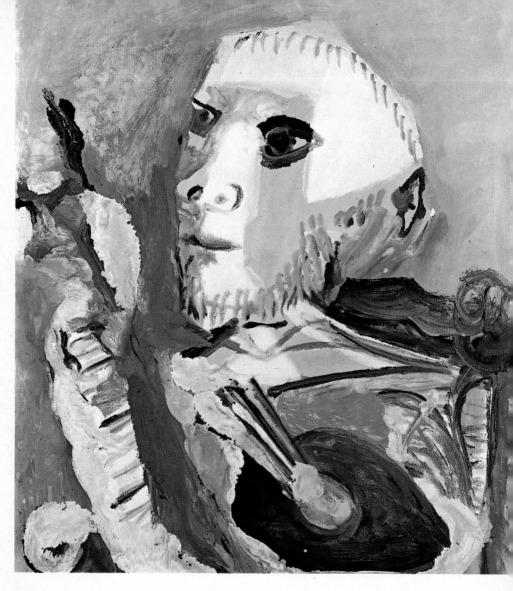

89 Autoportrait. 1965. Self-Portrait.